Worship of God as Mother

Mysticism of Devi Mahatmya

by
Swami Jyotirmayananda

YOGA RESEARCH FOUNDATION
(Non-profit Organization)

AIMS AND OBJECTS

1. To spread the laws of spiritual life.

2. To promote understanding of the unity of life among all people, regardless of race, sect, creed and sex, and also to promote harmony among all religions by emphasizing the fundamental unity of all prophets, saints, sages and teachers.

3. To help suffering humanity by teaching higher moral standards, prayers and meditation.

4. To give regular classes in the teachings of Yoga, Vedanta and Indian Philosophy.

5. To promote Universal Peace and Universal Love.

6. To promote the cultural growth of humanity on the basis of everlasting spiritual values of life.

7. To guide students and devotees all over the world.

8. To print and publish spiritual literature.

9. Anyone devoted to the ideals of truth, non-violence and purity can be a member of this Foundation.

© 2006 Swami Jyotirmayananda
All rights reserved.

Yoga Research Foundation
Mailing Address:
6111 S.W. 74th Avenue
Miami, Florida 33143
Tel: (305) 666-2006
www.yrf.org

ISBN 0-934664-53-6

Library of Congress Control Number: 2004107979

PRINTED IN THE UNITED STATES OF AMERICA

Worship of God as Mother

Mysticism of Devi Mahatmya

*Dedicated to
the Maha Devi—the Divine Mother
in Her three major aspects—
Durga, Lakshmi and Saraswati—
and to Her devotees, who are
like the blossoming flowers
wafting the fragrance of enlightenment
for the moral and spiritual
upliftment of humanity!*

Publisher's Note

This extraordinary book has been long awaited by many devotees. It contains the essence of the well known scripture—*Devi Mahatmya* or *Durga Shaptashati*, also known as *Chandi Path*. It is a portion from the *Markandeya Purana* written by Sage Vyasa.

Devi Mahatmya is a unique scripture that views God as Mother, and presents highly mystical stories depicting the journey of the soul from darkness to Light—from the misery of bondage to the Bliss of Liberation.

Many a battle must be fought, many an illusion must be broken, many rare qualities of head and heart must unfold, in order that the soul may reach its ultimate destination.in this process. An aspirant turns to the Goddess for guidance, support, removal of obstacles, endowment of divine virtues, and enlightenment.

As Durga, She destroys gross impurities urging the aspirant to develop purity of heart. As Lakshmi, She brings about the blossoming of divine qualities such as humility, truthfulness and fearlessness and frees the mind of distractions. As Saraswati, She destroys ignorance and egoism, and leads the soul to the heights of spiritual enlightenment.

In every manifestation, the Devi wages war against the forces of darkness. These stories yield fascinating insights into the mystery of life and the art of attaining spiritual evolution. Swami Jyotirmayananda, with his unique intuitive insight, has presented the mystical meanings of these stories, bringing to light the profound treasure that lies hidden in this great scripture.

The very concept of worshipping God as Mother has captured the head and heart of countless devotees not only in India, but in various parts of the world. In fact the Divine Self is sweeter than a thousand mothers, and mightier than a thousand fathers.

Every year, *Navaratri Puja* is performed in our ashram under the guidance of Swami Jyotirmayananda. During the serene hours of the morning, when the ashram garden softly emerges out of the blanket of darkness and is awakened by the song of birds, Swamiji conducts the most inspiring *puja* (worship). Each day Swamiji gives mystic insight into the stories of the Devi and their applications in daily life. Aspirants listen to the teachings, hear the inspiring songs and *kirtans* in praise of Devi, receive blessings from the Guru, and partake of delicious *prasad* (holy food). The present book contains the gems of teachings culled from these wonderful talks by Swamiji.

We are thankful to our ashram staff for their diligent work in doing all that is needed in bringing out this precious book—composing, proof-reading, graphic artistry, masking, preparing plates, printing and binding.

May the Goddess bestow Her blessings on the readers of this excellent book!

—Swami Lalitananda

This publication is dedicated:

*by Dr. Vasanti Puranik & Dr. Subhash Puranik
Plantation, Florida, USA
in memory of:*

*Govind Vyankatesh Puranik
Lakshmibai Govind Puranik
Jamkhandi, Bijapur, Maharashtra, India*

*Amritrao Tuljopant Phadnis
Ahilyabai Amritrao Phadnis
Aundh, Satara, Maharashtra, India*

*Ramachandra Govind Puranik
Seetadevi Ramachandra Puranik
Poona, Maharashtra, India*

*Vishvanath Keshav Joag
Gangabai Vishvanath Joag
Poona, Maharashtra, India*

*Shankar Ramachandra Kanitkar
Umabai Shankar Kanitkar
Poona, Maharashtra, India*

*Chintamani Vishvanath Joag
Kamal Chintamani Joag
Poona, Maharashtra, India*

Contents

The Glory of Mother Worship 11
   God as Mother 11
   Mother As Guide 12
   The Significance of Navaratri Worship 14
Listen to Me, Oh Beloved Mother (song lyrics) 19
From Darkness to Light—Mysticism of Mahakali in the Ratri Sukta of Rig Veda
   Oh Gentle Goddess (song lyrics) 24
   The Revelation of Ratri Sukta Elaborated into
      Durga Sapta-Shati 25
The All-Pervasive Mother 27
The Story Commences 33
   The Ashram of Sage Medha 34
   Verse for Meditation on Maha Kali 39
   Goddess as Durga 42
   Verse for Meditation on Maha Lakshmi 49
   Manifestation of Maha Lakshmi 52
      Destruction of Mahishasura 55
   Oh Mother, Goddess Durga (song lyrics) 64
   Verse for Meditation on Maha Saraswati 65
   Oh Goddess Lakshmi, Abide in My House (song lyrics) 68
   Manifestation of Maha Saraswati 69
      Destruction of Dhumralochana 72
      Destruction of Chanda and Munda 73
      Destruction of Raktabija 74
      Destruction of Nishumbha 83
      Destruction of Shumba 84

Oh Holy Mother, Touch Me (song lyrics) 88
Narayani Stuti (Adorations to Goddess Narayani) 92
The Glory of the Scripture 98
Conclusion of the Story 101

Turn Towards the Universal Mother 107
Relax in Her Divine Arms 113
The All-Compassionate Destroyer 116
The Plan of Navaratri Puja 118
Attainment of Spiritual Victory 125

Worship the Divine Mother Every Day of Your Life 127
Worship of Goddess Durga 127
Worship of Goddess Lakshmi 130
Worship of Goddess Saraswati 136

Prayer to Devi (song lyrics) 140

**Thoughts for Meditation on Each Night of
Mother Worship** 141
The Worship of Goddess Durga 141
The Worship of Goddess Lakshmi 146
The Worship of Goddess Saraswati 153
The Glory of Goddess 160

Prayers to Devi—the Cosmic Mother 162

Archana 165

Selections from Devi Sukta 168

Arati—The Waving of Light Ceremony 170

Oh Goddess Lakshmi, Smile Upon Me (song lyrics) 176

Chants for Auspiciousness 177

Oh Goddess Saraswati (song lyrics) 181

Meditation on the Mother as Energy 182

Oh Devi Durga (song lyrics) 185

**The Mysterious Ways of Maya (A parable adapted
from Devi Bhagavata)** 186

**The Rise and Fall of the Ego (A mystic story from
Devi Bhagavata)** 192

**Author
Sri Swami Jyotirmayananda**

The Glory of Mother Worship

God as Mother

The Divine Self or God has two aspects: Mother-aspect and Father-aspect. Truth, knowledge, power, infinity, justice, abstraction, sublimity, and suzerainty are qualities applied to the Father-aspect, while beauty, bliss, love, energy, luminosity, compassion, proximity, eternity and grace are the qualities of the Mother-aspect. These two aspects of God are worshipped by mankind in some fashion or other all over the world. The worship of the Mother-aspect is especially well-developed among the Hindus.

Most people think of God as a Father. However, the concept of God as Mother is more fulfilling because the love for mother in the depths of the heart is more deep-rooted than the love for father. No one can hold a secret from his mother. Sometimes a person has to seek the aid of his mother in order to please his father. Therefore, the concept of God as Mother is the most evolved expression of the religious feeling of a person towards the almighty God.

Even though God as the Mother is One, She manifests in various forms through the different stages of the evolution of the soul. Thus, She leads the infant soul along the path of *sadhana* or spiritual discipline with the aid of the Father. When the individual soul attains enlightenment and is freed of the cycles of birth and death, the Mother and the Father and the soul become one. This is Self-realization—that surging ocean wherein all dualities and multiplicities are dissolved and the fullness of bliss is experienced.

Mother as Guide

The Divine Mother trains the infant soul to balance its steps on the path of *sadhana* just as a mortal mother trains her baby with love and skill. The Divine Mother exists in a person in the depths of his being—in the innermost chamber of his heart. She is the original *Atma-shakti,* or energy of the Spirit that manifests in the form of *jnana shakti* (the energy of knowledge), *ichha shakti* (the energy of will and desire) and *kriya shakti* (the energy of action).

In the *Devi Mahatmya* the gods worshipped the Devi by the following hymns:

"Ya Devi sarvabhuteshu Vishnumayeti shabdita,
Namastasyai, namastasyai, namastasyai namo namah"

(Prostrations to that Devi who is called Vishnu Maya among all creatures— prostrations, prostrations!)

Then the *devas* (gods) go on describing the Devi in a similar way:

"Salutations, again and again salutations, to Her Who is known among all beings as consciousness, as intellect, as hunger, as shadow, as power, as thirst, as forbearance, as caste, as shyness, as grace, as faith, as beauty, as prosperity, as effort, as memory, as mercy, as contentment, as Mother, as delusion, and Who is called among human beings the sustainer of all. To Her, let our salutations be given!"

The above prayer describes the different manifestations of the Devi. The life of a person is permeated by these manifestations. The Mother guides Her child, the spiritual aspirant, internally and externally. The entire *prakriti* (nature) is Her sporting grounds and all the manifestations of the world, including the earth and the heavens, are Her glories. Her divine ways of guiding the infant soul are mysterious. She is frightful and terrible as Durga, destroying the obstacles that rise from the *tamasic* or demoniac level. She is lustrous as Lakshmi—the bestower of material and spiritual wealth. In the form of Saraswati, She is most sublime and elegant as She rides on the mystic swan, conferring the knowledge that leads to immortality.

The Divine Mother has innumerable manifestations. Sometimes She is terrible, sometimes compassionate, sometimes tempting and alluring, sometimes seducing and deceiving, sometimes threatening and overpowering, sometimes sublime and elevating. The same Mother puts on different veils during the different conditions in the evolution of the soul to aid its Godward movements. How compassionate, how motherly!

The Significance of Navaratri Worship

In India, *Navaratri Puja* (Mother Worship) is celebrated in the bright half of the lunar month of *Ashwina* (September-October). The Mother aspect of God is worshipped as Durga, Lakshmi, and Saraswati, each for three nights respectively. This time is propitious because the rains have ceased in India and the sky is placid and clear, with the stars shining gently. Cool, fresh, and fragrant breezes blow all over India. It is in such an elegant setting of nature that one is reminded of the glory of the Divine Mother. Therefore, it is suitable that the *Puja* be performed by innumerable devotees all over India in recognition of the compassion of the Mother-aspect of God, so that they may draw Her grace on their spiritual path towards liberation. The *Puja* of the

Mother puts an end to the torrents of the afflictions and renders the firmament of the heart free from the dark clouds of karmas.

Navaratri Puja depicts the long course of spiritual evolution in the life of the *sadhaka* (spiritual aspirant) and reveals the way in which the Divine Mother leads the soul to the ultimate victory over the *asuric* and *rakshasic* qualities (demoniac qualities) which present countless obstacles on the spiritual path. *Navaratri Puja* culminates on the tenth day, which is called *Vijaya Dashami*. The tenth day celebrates the victory of the Devi over the demons. *Vijaya Dashami* also commemorates Rama's victory over Ravana. Sri Rama, the great incarnation of Vishnu, attained victory over Ravana (symbolic of ignorance) and paved the way for *Rama Rajya* (liberation).

In a *sadhaka's* life, the forces of darkness manifest as anger and hatred, malice and greed, pride and infatuation, craving and conceit, etc. On the other hand, the forces of light manifest as compassion and magnanimity, humility and charity, purity and sincerity, universal love and peace. Life is an arena for the battling forces of darkness and light. The essence of the *Puja* is to enhance the forces of light, to control the senses and the mind, to overcome the desires emanating from the lower self, and to realize the Self that shines in the cave of the heart.

It has been already pointed out that the Mother-aspect of God is manifested in three different aspects in the three phases of *sadhana*. In the first stage, the heart of the aspirant is tainted by the impurities of innumerable births. The *malas* or impurities of the heart express themselves in the form of anger, greed, hatred, lust, pride, jealousy, etc. Those *malas* represent the demoniac forces in a person. They are verily demons like Madhu, Kaitabha, Mahisha, Shumbha and Nishumbha. The Durga-aspect of the Divine Mother is worshipped for the destruction and sublimation of those impurities. Goddess Durga, therefore, is the terrible aspect of the Mother whose Divine power is awe-inspiring in the heart of a person.

Goddess Lakshmi is worshipped in the second stage. Lakshmi is the goddess of wealth and prosperity. She is symbolic of divine glory or *aishwarya*. This phase of *sadhana* is marked by the development of divine qualities such as compassion, dispassion, purity, renunciation, charity, universal love, unity, magnanimity of the heart, balance of mind, etc. These are rare gifts of spiritual wealth. Goddess Lakshmi brings steadiness in the *chitta* (mind stuff) by enriching the spirit. *Vikshepa* (distraction of mind) is removed in this phase.

Goddess Saraswati, or the Goddess of Knowledge, is worshipped in the third stage. While Durga rides on a lion, which is the symbol of willpower, Saraswati rides on a *hamsa* or swan, which is the symbol of the power of knowledge or discrimination. While Durga holds blazing weapons in Her innumerable hands as the symbol of struggle and destruction in the physical plane, and Lakshmi holds a blossoming lotus flower as a symbol of spiritual unfoldment and divine prosperity in the astral plane, Saraswati holds a *veena* in Her hands that symbolizes the harmony of perfection.

In the state of such Divine harmony, the discordant notes of the personality are tuned so perfectly that the music of the soul flows uninterruptedly as it silences the discordant notes of the senses and the noises of the world. Saraswati is the symbol of knowledge that tears the veil of ignorance or *avarana* and reveals the splendor of Consciousness. The realization of the unveiled beauty of the Supreme confers immortality.

Let us pray to the Divine Mother from the depths of our hearts:

*Oh Mother, when shalt Thou
bestow upon us dispassion
and devotion to Thy lotus feet?
How long shall we suffer from
the afflictions of samsara (world-process)?
How long shall we remain deluded
due to Thy innumerable enchantments?*

*Let us behold Thee in all, especially in all women,
who are Thy special manifestations.
Let us waft the fragrance of purity in
thought, word, and deed.
Let us awaken the sleeping kundalini and
take Thee to the sahasrara, where, oh Mother,
Thou art united with Shiva or the Absolute!*

*Oh compassionate Mother,
Thou art the ocean of energy.
Bestow upon us the power of sadhana,
the power of inquiry,
the power of discrimination,
so that we may become One with Thee
and enter along with Thee into the Absolute.*

LISTEN TO ME
OH BELOVED MOTHER

Oh holy Mother,
Oh holy Mother,
Help me, help me.
If you do not help me,
Who will find me?
Listen to me, oh beloved Mother.
I have fallen like a star from the sky
Into the Ocean of misery.
You must hear,
Oh holy Mother,
Oh holy Mother.

Oh Mother,
Make me well from head to toe
With prana shining bright.
May my mind be ever pure
like the sparkling streams
Of the hills of Kashmir
In the morning sun.
May my heart be as kind
As the sweet lillies of early spring.

Oh gracious Mother,
May my soul be expansive
Like the infinite blue sky.
I beseech you, my holy Mother,
Perform your Divine miracle
And make me free to merge and melt
Like a ray of sun in your Cosmic heart.

Oh holy Mother, oh holy Mother.
You must hear my cry.
I am so near.

May my mind be ever pure
Like the sparkling streams
Of the hills of Kashmir
In the morning sun.
May my heart be as kind
As the sweet lillies of early spring.

Oh holy Mother, oh holy Mother.

Song Lyrics & Music
by Swami Lalitananda

From Darkness to Light

Mysticism of Mahakali in the Ratri Sukta of Rig Veda

The plan of *Durga Sapta-Shati* (the scripture dealing with Mother Worship) finds its roots in the Ratri Sukta, a hymn from the Rig Veda in praise of the Goddess of Night. Here is a simple version of that hymn which was revealed by Sage Bharadwaja:

Om. The all-pervading Devi, having created the jivas (individual souls) of this universe, expresses Her numerous glories in order to provide fruits for their karmas. 1

This Goddess is immortal; She permeates this universe; She encompasses the creepers (of the forests of the world) that grow downwards, as well as the trees that grow upwards. She destroys darkness by the Light of Wisdom. 2

The Goddess of Night, Who is pure consciousness, having manifested, reveals Her sister Usha (the Goddess of Dawn), Who destroys the darkness of ignorance. 3

May that Goddess of Night be propitious for us! It is by Her advent that we sleep soundly in our homes, much in the same way as birds repose joyously in their nests. 4

In the loving arms of the Goddess, all human beings, cows, horses and other animals, birds that fly in the air, such as the hawks and others, and even the moths and other small creatures—all sleep peacefully. 5

Oh Goddess of Night! May Thou be gracious to free me from the she-wolf of vasanas (the subtle desires based upon ignorance and egoism) and the he-wolf of sinful karmas; Free me from thieves (in the form of anger, hatred and others), and lead me across the world-process. Become, Thou, the bestower of Liberation! 6

Oh Usha (the Goddess of Dawn)—the presiding Deity of the night! This all encompassing darkness has enveloped me from all sides. You who relieve Your devotees of their burdens by paying their debts, may You relieve us of ignorance. 7

Oh Goddess of Night! Thou art like a milch-cow (the nourisher of the soul and the giver of desired objects). Having approached Thee, I seek Thy Grace by offering my prayers unto Thee. Oh daughter of the luminous sky (the Ether of the Self), by Thy Grace I have conquered my enemies (anger, hate and others). May Thou accept my offerings! 8

Mystic Meaning

The richness of the spiritual imagery expressed in these earliest revelations is boundless. The predicament of the soul as it journeys through the world-process is compared to the predicament of a traveller who has wandered away from home and finds himself lost in a forest during the darkness of the night.

But instead of being confounded by the darkness that seems to engulf him, he discovers a mystic insight. He realizes that there is a Divine Basis behind that terrifying darkness. This darkness of the night, which offers terrifying conditions for those who are lost, is also the giver of rest and peace to all living beings. It is due to the grace of that dark night that all living beings go to sleep, even as infants rest in the arms of their mothers.

Esoterically speaking, the dark night is symbolic of *Maya Shakti*—the Power of Cosmic Illusion. The souls are encompassed by the dark night of *Maya*.

Led by their karmas they wander from one embodiment to another. During this process, the Divine Mother, assuming the role of ignorance, provides comfort and solace to them in a negative manner.

As long as spiritual insight has not dawned, ignorance keeps a person oblivious of the manifold miseries that encompass him from all sides. Thus, the force of ignorance and delusion is of importance in one's spiritual evolution. Just as a person with weak eyesight needs to keep his eyes protected by colored glass, in the same manner, by creating the veils of illusion, the Goddess keeps the tender vision of Her children shielded against the glaring Light of the Self.

However, just as the dark night glides on to a state of golden dawn, in the same manner, when the Goddess of Night is propitiated, She assumes a different aspect—She becomes the Goddess of Dawn. The dark clouds that seemed terrifying now become transformed into silvery clouds, and are decked with

colorful robes woven by the rays of light. What wonderous transformation the Goddess of Dawn brings in the firmament of the sky!

O GENTLE GODDESS

The cold winter night has fallen,
The demons appear in dark trees.
Alone I pray, alone I wait.
O gentle Goddess,
Touch me with your goodness,
Touch me with your beauty.

When midnight comes,
My soul stands still,
Afraid you may not appear—
Yet knowing you will come out of
Compassion for my plight.

Alone I pray,
Alone I wait.
Om Aim Saraswatyai Namaha.

The curtain moves,
The winter is gone
And the dawn of spring steps
through my window.
You are here with me at last.
O gentle Goddess,
Touch me with your goodness,
Touch me with your beauty.

Song Lyrics & Music by Swami Lalitananda

The Revelation of Ratri Sukta Elaborated into Durga Sapta-Shati

Durga Sapta-Shati is a *tantric* text devoted to the worship of God as Mother *(Shakti)*. It is a profound spiritual text that presents the art of worshipping *Shakti*, and tells a thrilling story of how *Shakti* assumes Her different roles and destroys the demoniac impediments from the path of a spiritual aspirant. Then, having led the aspirant to the state of Enlightenment, She becomes One with the Absolute Self (Shiva).

This above plan of moving from the darkness of night to the unfoldment of light through dawn is presented by Nature day by day, and has become the basis for the spiritual plan outlined in Mother Worship. The terrible darkness of the night passes through three prominent stages: 1. The dense darkness represented by Kali or Durga 2. The movement towards dawn when the clouds become rich with dazzling colors of gold and silver, represented by Goddess Lakshmi, and 3. The dawn ushering in the glorious sunrise, represented by Goddess Saraswati— the giver of Knowledge. Thus, the Deity of the Night, having led the aspirant to the golden sunrise, vanishes from view, as if She Herself has become merged into the ocean of Light.

In the same manner, on the spiritual path an aspirant first seeks the grace of Goddess Maha Kali for the removal of gross impurities (such as anger, greed and others). He then becomes aware of the grace of Goddess Lakshmi, which results in his personality becoming decked with divine virtues. That is, his unconscious, which was filled with the dark clouds of impure impressions, now becomes a storehouse of divine impressions—of goodness, spiritual expansion and divine virtues. The dark clouds have thus been transformed into the clouds of predawn, into angels of light. This stage is mystically elaborated into the worship of Goddess Lakshmi.

Finally there arrives the Dawn in Her luminous attire, Who sweeps the sky of all its darkness with the broom of Her luminous rays. So too, when an aspirant has attained purity of heart and has developed divine wealth, he begins to experience the transformation of reason into intuition. Goddess Saraswati is the embodiment of this light of intuition. She is the giver of Knowledge. She is the source of all artistic and creative inspirations that are the basis for all that is good and wonderful in the world. And at last, Dawn disappears and the Sun (the Absolute Self, *Para Shakti* or *Brahman*) shines, illumining all.

Thus, the Goddess, having removed gross impurities in the form of Maha Kali, having decked the aspirant with the wealth of divine virtues as Maha Lakshmi, and having led him to the state of intuitional vision as Maha Saraswati, merges Herself in *Brahman*, the Absolute Self.

The All-Pervasive Mother

*T*he whole universe is the sportive manifestation of the Divine Being in the Mother-aspect. The Divine Mother permeates the whole world. She is within and around us, functioning in the intellect as *jnana shakti* or the energy of knowledge, in the mind as *ichha shakti* or the energy of desire or will, and in the physical body as *kriya shakti* or the energy of action.

There are many names that are synonymous for the Divine Mother. These include: *Devi* or Goddess; *Mata* or Mother; *Maya* or the principle of Cosmic Illusion, which is inseparable from *Brahman* or the Absolute ; *Moola Prakriti* or the balanced state of the three *gunas* (the three modes of nature—*sattwa, rajas* and *tamas*).

Mother Worship is as old as the instinctive human feeling of love for one's mother, as old as life in the human plane. This form of worship enables a spiritual aspirant to feel and experience the compassionate hand of the Mother-aspect of God behind every event of his life. The Mother presents *bhoga* (the enjoyments of the world) and *moksha* (the infinite bliss of liberation) to every individual soul.

Devi or the Goddess assumes a deluding aspect to those who are in lesser planes of evolution—those who have not yet been drawn to the higher values of life and are, therefore, entangled in worldly enjoyments. She deludes them in such a way that they ignorantly believe that their impure physical body is the pure Self. They are also deluded into the belief that their transitory life is eternal, that the painful enjoyments of the world are blissful, and that their inert mind and intellect are the conscious Self. This deluding aspect of the Goddess is called *avidya* or ignorance.

The compassionate Mother awaits the return of every one of Her children, or individual souls, from the world-process. Even while Her delusive force has its sway, Her compassion towards every one of Her children is unfailing. No matter how far one may wander in the forest of the world-process, one is never far away from the Divine Mother. One is ever enfolded in Her arms.

A baby sleeping on the lap of his mother may have unpleasant dreams; yet on waking he sees his mother smiling and realizes that he has been all the time enfolded by her tender care. He does not realize all this, however, until he wakes up. Similarly, every soul is being held in the compassionate hands of the Goddess, and She is closer to us than our very breath, closer than our very heart. This is so because She is the material out of which the intellect, the mind, and the senses have been fashioned. Yet, due to ignorance, one experiences a sense of separation from the Mother through the long dream of *samsara*, the world-process.

Those who are pure in heart and who have turned away from the world-process, the seekers of nectar, the spiritual aspirants after liberation—in them the Goddess manifests Her *vidya* aspect or the aspect of knowledge that unveils the myriad beauties of the Supreme and reveals the profundity of Divine glory in every object of the world. The patient effort with which Nature strives to awaken every soul from the long dream of *samsara* is indescribable. It is a patience that only a mother could possess!

Mother Worship is also related to *shakti upasana*, or the worship of energy or power. A worshipper of *shakti* or energy realizes that without strength there is neither enjoyment nor liberation. Such a worshipper thus prays to the Mother for increasing strength on all levels of his personality. The strength of the body is inferior to the strength of the mind, the strength of the mind is inferior to the strength of the intellect, and the strength of the intellect is inferior to the strength of the soul. By allowing the grace of the Goddess to operate through his entire being, a worshipper of *shakti* eventually becomes endowed with immense strength of the soul or spirit. With this strength, he attains liberation and merges into the Absolute.

Scriptures such as *Devi Mahatmya* or the Glory of the Mother, *Devi Bhagavata, Markandeya Purana,* and various *Upanishads* dealing with the glory of the Mother contain most enchanting and profound stories about the Divine Goddess and the different manifestations that She uses for the destruction of demons, and for the bestowal of boons to devotees.

The demons, whose evil aspects are so colorfully described in the scriptures, represent the forces of darkness hidden in every human being in the form of attachment, hatred, pride, conceit, egoism, jealousy, greed, passion and the many vices that arise out of ignorance. The gods, with their graceful forms moving in aerial cars and sporting in the heavenly gardens, represent the forces of light operating through every being in the form of love, compassion, patience, selflessness, purity, renunciation, fearlessness, detachment, discrimination, and other virtues that spring from wisdom and illumination.

How does the Universal Mother intervene in the battles of the two forces and bring about the victory of light over darkness? This has been most figuratively and mystically described in the stories of the Devi. Those who have insight into human life and into the Divine force that operates through it will marvel at the exquisite intuitional vision of the sages who, full of compassion, presented to the world these stories of Devi—stories garbed in an excellent poetic language and ornamented with mystic imagery that make Her battles with the demons so fascinating for an aspirant.

Just as the Goddess manifests in the external universe as the destroyer in the form of Durga, as the granter of prosperity in the form of Lakshmi, and as the bestower of talent, creativity and knowledge in the form of Saraswati, even so, She manifests internally in each individual as the terrible Durga for the removal of all obstacles, as the graceful Lakshmi for the revival of divine qualities, and as the luminous Saraswati to bring illumination and dispel the darkness of *avidya* or ignorance.

From the spiritual point of view, every event is a wave in the Absolute. The external and internal aspects are forms of the Absolute. To those who have acquired spiritual vision, the world is nothing but *Brahman* or the Absolute. They are free from any battle because they are established in nonduality.

Because of our frail and finite intellects, we have no right to deny the historicity of the great descriptions of the heroic acts of Devi. However, all these marvels are but little in comparison to what the Divine Mother is doing in every moment of our existence. The world with all its incredible beauty gives only a mere hint of the glory and majesty of the Mother. You can imagine, then, how glorious and how beautiful the Mother must be!

We now proceed to give you a condensed narration of the stories of the glorious deeds of the Devi with their esoteric meaning so that you may pursue the most meaningful form of *Devi puja* or worship of the Cosmic Mother.

The Story Commences

The Ashram of Sage Medha

*I*n ancient days there ruled a heroic and powerful king named Suratha. He was magnanimous, righteous, dutiful, and truthful. During his reign, many great kings became his enemies, and it came to pass that their armies surrounded the capital of Suratha. In the battle that ensued, Suratha was defeated because his own ministers had turned against him. They misappropriated the treasury and all the king's possessions. In order to save his life, the King had to run away into a dense forest. Wandering in the forest, he saw the hermitage of a great sage named Medha.

Through the benign influence of Sage Medha, the wild animals there had given up their antagonism and were living in perfect harmony. The King was welcomed by the Sage and lived in his *ashrama*. One day a *vaishya* or merchant came into the *ashrama*. The King noticed that this *vaishya* was troubled and asked him why this was so. The *vaishya* replied:

"Oh King, I am a *vaishya* and my name is Samadhi. I was born in a rich family, but my wife and my relatives threw me out of my house due to their greed for wealth. I have thus wandered in this forest and have come to this *ashrama*. I have not been able to get any news from my wife, children, grandsons, brothers, or other relatives. I am broken-hearted."

The King replied: "Oh Samadhi, why are you still thinking about those who expelled you from your house? You are acting foolishly." Samadhi said: "Oh King, I know that you are telling me the truth, but still I am chained to them by affection. My mind is deluded."

Eager to receive guidance, Suratha and Samadhi went to Sage Medha to ask for his help in breaking the chains that tied their hearts to the objects of the world. Folding his hands in adoration, the king asked:

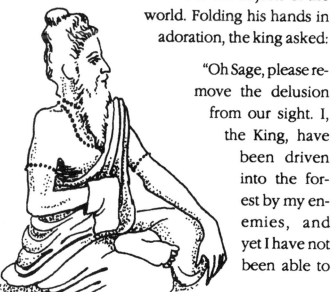

"Oh Sage, please remove the delusion from our sight. I, the King, have been driven into the forest by my enemies, and yet I have not been able to renounce the thoughts of my kingdom. This *vaishya*, Samadhi, has been driven off by his own relatives and has not been able to renounce his affection towards them. Though we are both intelligent, we are not able to remove the ties of affection and the clouds of delusion from our vision."

Sage Medha replied: "Oh King, there is a beginningless power known as Jagadamba, the Mother of the Universe. It is She who draws the minds of people and deludes them. Deluded by Her *maya*, even Gods are not able to know the highest, let alone mortals. The Goddess appears in various forms through the three modes of nature or *gunas (sattwa, rajas and tamas)* and carries out the works of creation, sustenance, and dissolution of the universe. Only those who please the Devi can cross the ocean of delusion.

It is due to the delusive power of the Goddess that all living beings behave in such strange ways. See how tenderly a mother vulture feeds her young ones. But when they grow up she has nothing more to do with them. Much in the same manner, deluded by *Maya*, human beings develop attachment and hatred, and therefore continue to whirl through cycles of birth and death by maintaining karmic bondage. But there is a divine art through which one can overcome the delusive power of the Goddess and break the fetters of karma. One needs to take refuge in the Goddess Herself, who has Herself spread the veils of illusion before his eyes."

Mystic Meaning

Suratha literally means "one who is endowed with a good chariot." Suratha stands for the *jivatman* or the individual soul, which is endowed with the chariot of the body. The individual soul is chained to the world-process by various attachments and *karmic* entanglements. The soul indulges in worldly pleasures because it has forgotten its essential nature—*Brahman* (the Absolute Self).

In the course of time, having passed through numerous embodiments, it develops *vairagya* or dispassion, and realizes its miserable predicament. It gains an insight into the fact that even the closest relatives of the world cannot come to its aid in the hours of suffering. Nowhere in the world of time and space can the soul find true repose and lasting happiness. Finding pain and misery everywhere, the individual soul goes to the hermitage of Medha Rishi. Medha literally means "the purified intellect" or "the intuitive intellect." The individual soul seeks the guidance of the intuitive intellect.

Samadhi is the state in which the mind is free from thought-waves. It is the power of the soul by which the senses are withdrawn from the sense-objects. Just as *vaishyas* (the merchant class) tend cows and have the power to control them, even so does Samadhi have the power of controlling the senses and mind. That is why Samadhi is called a *vaishya*. When the mind is engaged in external objects and actions, the state of *samadhi* is veiled. Samadhi is as if ignored by his own relatives and friends—the numerous thoughts of the mind.

When Suratha (the individual soul) joins Samadhi (a *vaishya*) and approaches the hermitage of Medha Rishi (the intuitive intellect), it attains the revelation of the Cosmic Mother and regains the lost empire of the Self (God-realization).

Medha Rishi or the purified intellect guides the soul through the various stages of spiritual battle and gives insights into the powers that assist it in those stages. These insights and teachings are presented in the profoundly mystical stories of the Goddess.

Verse for Meditation on Maha Kali (Goddess Durga)

ॐ खड्गं चक्रगदेषुचापपरिघान् शूलं भुशुण्डीं शिरः
शङ्खं सन्दधतीं करैस्त्रिनयनां सर्वाङ्गभूषावृताम् ।
यां हन्तुं मधुकैटभौ जलजभूस्तुष्टावसप्ते हरौ
नीलाश्मद्युतिमास्यपाददशकां सेवे महाकालिकाम् ॥

Om khadgam chakragadeshu-chaap-paridhaan shoolam bhushundeem shirah. Shankham sandadhateem karaistrinayanaam sarvaanga-bhooshavritaam. Yaam hantum madhukaitabho jalajabhoostusbtaavasapte harau Neelashmadytimaasya-paadadashakaam sevemahaa-kaalikaam.

"I adore that Mahakali, Who was invoked by the lotus-born Brahma while Lord Vishnu slept, for the destruction of Madhu and Kaitabha. I adore that Goddess who holds in Her hands a sword, discus, mace, arrow, bow, club, spears, missiles, a human skull, and a conch; Who has three eyes and is adorned with the divine ornaments; Who is luminous like a blue jewel, and who has ten faces and ten legs."

Mystic Meaning

Goddess Kali is portrayed as the Goddess with ten faces, ten legs and twenty arms riding on a lion. She is the symbol of Maya Shakti (the Goddess presiding over Cosmic Illusion) in the aspect of "the destroyer."

On the spiritual path, an aspirant needs to overcome the gross impurities that keep his mind clouded. These impurities are the various ramifications of *raga* or attachment (symbolized by the Demon Madhu) and *dwesha* or hatred (symbolized by the Demon Kaitabha).

The various weapons of the Goddess are symbolic of numerous forms of energy that proceed from the Goddess towards creation, sustenance and dissolution of the world.

The sword is the symbol of purified intellect. The discus is righteousness that is bound to triumph over all that is unrighteous. The mace pulverizes the obstacles on the path. The bow is the purified *chitta* (mind-stuff) that sends out arrows of dynamic thoughts for destroying the forces of darkness. The club is unshakable willpower, the spear is insight, the missile is intuitive knowledge. The skull is symbolic of increasing dispassion, and the conch heralds the rising of wisdom. The Divine ornaments that adorn Her are symbolic of spiritual virtues such as truth, purity, contentment, compassion, knowledge, devotion, and others which deck the soul of Her devotee with the imperishable wealth of spiritual values.

Her many faces, legs and arms are symbolic of Her boundless energy and all-pervasiveness. The human skull in the hands of the Goddess symbolizes not only the need of dispassion on the spiritual path, but also the fact that all objects of this world are perishable and even the very universe itself is subject to destruction.

Her complexion shines like a blue-jewel, and is symbolic of the fact that She is the Deity presiding over the "dark night" of the soul. When propitiated, She leads the soul to Her gentle aspect—Lakshmi Devi (the Goddess of Prosperity)—and then to Her most luminous aspect—Saraswati Devi (the Goddess of Wisdom).

Goddess as Durga

The King asked: "Who is the Devi Who deludes all? Please tell me Her story and Her sportive plays so that I may be enlightened."

Medha, the sage, continued: Oh King, during the *pralaya* or cosmic deluge, great Lord Vishnu was sleeping soundly on the couch of the Shesha serpent. There was water everywhere. From the ears of Lord Vishnu emerged two demons named Madhu and Kaitabha. They had gigantic forms and were as luminous as the sun. They were also terrible like death. When they saw Brahma, the creator, seated on a lotus flower that had risen from the navel of Lord Vishnu, the two demons thundered at Brahma, "Who are you?" They immediately wanted to kill him.

Sensing the danger to his life and seeing that Lord Vishnu was still asleep, Brahma started to pray to the Goddess: "Oh Mother of the Universe, please delude these demons and awaken the Lord from His slumber."

Goddess Durga then arose from every limb of Lord Vishnu and appeared before Brahma riding on a Lion. She had many arms, and in each hand She was holding a dazzling weapon or an auspicious object. She said: "Oh Creator, do not be afraid.

Today I shall destroy the demons Madhu and Kaitabha and free you from your troubles."

When Devi awakened the Lord from His slumber, He saw the valiant demons before Him and fought with them for five thousand celestial years. Being deluded by *Maha Maya,* the Great Goddess, the demons said to the Lord: "We are pleased with Your fight. Please accept a boon from us."

Lord Vishnu said: "If it pleases you, then give Me the boon that both of you may be killed by My hands." The demons said, "You may kill us only in a place where there is no water." Lord Vishnu said, "May it be so," and placing their heads on His thighs

that were above the waters, He cut off their heads with His effulgent discus.

This is the story of the manifestation of the Goddess Durga or Kalika or Mahakali, the terrible aspect of the Mother. Although the Mother does not have any form or attribute, She does assume a different form in different ages to relieve Her devotees of their miseries and to establish order in the world. The devotees sing the glory of each of the manifestations of the Devi. They meditate upon the divine form of the Devi and attain union with Her. Thus, they transcend the world-process and enjoy everlasting Bliss.

Mystic Meaning

In this first portion of the story of the Goddess, Lord Vishnu's sleep is symbolic of the fact that *Brahman*, or the Absolute Self, is ever untouched by, or detached from, the world-process. He alone is.

The *pralaya* state is the state of dissolution of the world when the three *gunas* or the modes of nature (*sattwa*—harmony and purity, *rajas*—passion and restless activity, *tamas*—inertia and darkness) are in perfect balance.

The water referred to in the story is the *avyaktam* or the non-manifest (the causal water) in which the seeds of future creations lie hidden. The Shesha serpent which serves as a couch for Lord Vishnu symbolizes the Cosmic Mind or the infinity aspect of the Lord, and the hoods of the Shesha serpent represent the countlesss powers of the Divinity.

Human misery throughout the cycles of birth and death is caused by *avidya* (ignorance), which in turn promotes the formation of attachment *(raga)* and hatred *(dwesha)* in the mind of the individual. These two major afflictions, respectively symbolized by the Demon Madhu, (literally meaning honey), and the Demon Kaitabha (meaning that which is bitter), arose out of the impurities of the ears of Vishnu— indicating that when one lacks the mystic art of listening to the teachings of the scriptures, he allows these two demons to dominate his mind.

When the mind is dominated by these two demons, the individual loses the sense of creativity that exists within. That is, the latent "Brahma" in the individual falls prey to demoniac forces such as anger, lust, greed, pride, jealousy and others.

In the first stage of *sadhana*, these impressions of *raga* and *dwesha*, which are the seeds of future births, must be destroyed. It is Durga or Kalika Devi, the terrific manifestation of the Goddess, who appears in the first stage of an aspirant's spiritual life to destroy these gross obstacles. This is why the Devi is portrayed as riding on a lion, which symbolizes bravery and power. The numerous weapons in the hands of the Devi are different spiritual powers assisting the aspirant in destroying the gross impurities of his heart.

Through devotion, Durga Devi is pleased, and the Divine Vishnu, Who was as if asleep, is awakened. This is symbolic of the awakening of mystical power in an aspirant through the practice of listening, reflection and meditation. Thus awakened, the soul of the aspirant fights its battle against *mala*—the gross impurities of the mind (represented by Madhu and Kaitabha) and attains victory over them. The victory over *raga* and *dwesha* is the beginning of the spiritual movement that culminates in the cessation of the world-process through the attainment of Self-realization.

It must be further understood that an individual cannot destroy these impurities by force. They have to be led to a plane which is beyond the realms (waters) of the world-process. This is the plane of the purified *chitta* (mind), which is represented by the thighs of Lord Vishnu, where the forces of darkness are destroyed by the shining rays of intuitive knowledge (the discus of Lord Vishnu).

Without the function of *Maya Shakti*, Brahman cannot become the destroyer of *raga* and *dwesha*, and without their destruction an aspirant cannot progress on the spiritual path. Vishnu is the Immutable Self, and the Goddess is the *Maya Shakti*—the power of Cosmic Illusion. Just as fire and heat, ice and coolness, are inseparable, so too *Brahman* and *Maya* are inseparable. Just as fire cannot work without heat, in the same way Lord Vishnu cannot work without the Goddess. Thus, the importance of *Maya Shakti* is to be understood in all its clarity.

By directing his devotion to *Maya Shakti* and by surrendering to her all-encompassing presence, an aspirant learns the secret of spiritual progress. The very same power of delusion now becomes a liberating force, and the Dark Night shows Her colorful aspect as She proceeds to the stage of the Golden Dawn.

So, even in the midst of the encircling gloom of confusion and despair, an aspirant is able to feel the presence of the Goddess. And once this awareness develops, a unique joy surges in his heart—for behind Her terrifying mask, he has seen the compassionate eyes of the Mother.

The destruction of Madhu and Kaitabha marks the piercing of *Brahma granthi*—the knot of Brahma located in the *Manipura Chakra* in the navel region. When the impressions of *raga* and *dwesha* are destroyed, the spiritual aspirant is endowed with dispassion. This knot is also termed as *Karma Granthi* or the knot of *karma* in the vedantic scriptures. The destruction of Madhu and Kaitabha leads to the realization of the *Sat* (Existence) aspect of *Brahman*. At this stage the *kundalini shakti* has pierced the *Manipura Chakra* and is ready to proceed to the higher *chakras*.

This, in brief, is the story of the Goddess in the role of Mother Kali, who is also known as Durga Devi. May the Goddess remove all obstacles from the path leading to Self-realization and shower upon us Her infinite blessings!

Mantras for the propitiation of the Devi in her terrific aspect of Kali or Durga:

Om Namashchandikaayai

Om Aim Hreem Kleem Chaamundaayai Vicche

This *mantra* suggests the following mystical meaning: "O Goddess! You are the embodiment of Existence, Knowledge and Bliss Absolute. Desirous of attaining knowledge of the Absolute Self, we meditate upon You. Adorations to You, O Chandika, who manifests as Maha Kali, Maha Lakshmi and Maha Saraswati. May You remove the fetters of ignorance and lead us to liberation!"

Om Sri Durgaayai Namah

Verse for Meditation on Maha Lakshmi:

ॐ अक्षसक्परशुं गदेषुकुलिशं पद्मं धनुष्कुण्डिकां
दण्डं शक्तिमसिं च चर्म जलजं घण्टां सुराभाजनं ।
शूलं पाशसुदर्शने च दधतीं हस्तैः प्रसन्ननानां
सेवे सैरिभमर्दिनीमिह महालक्ष्मीं सरोजस्थिताम् ॥

Om akshasrak-parashum gadeshu-kulisham padmam dhanushkundikaam. Dandam shaktimasim cha charma jalajam ghantaam suraabhaajanam. Shoolam paasha-sudarshane cha dadhateem hastaih prasannaananaam. Seve sairibhamardineemiha mahaalakshmeem sarojasthitaam.

I worship Goddess Mahalakshmi who is seated on the lotus, of cheerful face, the destroyer of the demon Mahishasura, who holds in her (eighteen) hands rosary, axe, mace, arrow, thunderbolt, lotus, bow, pitcher, rod, spear, sword, shield, conch, bell, wine-cup, trident, noose and the discus (Sudarshana).

Mystic Meaning

The spirit of distraction is symbolized as Mahishasura—the demon who appears in the form of a buffalo. The seat of lotus is the symbol of unfoldment. With the advent of Mahalakshmi, an aspirant begins to conquer the distractions of his mind, which have their roots in the subtle desires of the unconscious, and then, the divine potentiality begins to blossom like the lotus.

Her many hands symbolize her numerous powers. Devotion is symbolized by rosary. Axe is the wisdom by which an aspirant cuts down the tree of the world-process. Mace is the strength of purity by which the obstacles on the spiritual path are pulverized. Pure thoughts emerge from the mind, even like arrows of the Devi, for destroying the painful thoughtwaves of the mind.

The indomitable faith of the aspirant is the thunderbolt of the Devi. Virtuous qualities bloom like lotuses. Purified *chitta* (the mind-stuff) is the bow through which powerful thoughts are discharged like arrows. Pitcher refers to the *shubha samskaras* (divine impressions) of the unconscious mind. Rod is the symbol of discriminative knowledge that endows the intellect with a special power. *Shakti* or spear is the power that penetrates the heart of negative qualities and destroys them.

Her sword removes delusions of the mind, and Her shield protects the devotee from the forces of darkness. Conch is the awakener of divine potentiality, and bell is the revealer of spiritual insight. Wine-cup holds the bliss of *samadhi* (superconsciousness). Trident destroys the triads—the three aspects of the relative world (time, space, and causation). Noose stops the activity of the demoniac qualities, and discus Sudarshana slays the very root of all evils—ignorance.

Manifestation of Maha Lakshmi

*I*n ancient times a demon known as Mahishasura rose to a mighty power. He was given a boon from Brahma, the creator, that only a woman could kill him. He cleverly thought that he had attained immortality because he did not think that there would ever be a woman that could kill him.

Indra was the ruler of the gods. A fight that lasted for a hundred celestial years ensued between the gods and the demons who were headed by Mahishasura. The valiant demons overpowered the gods, and Mahishasura acquired the throne of Indra.

Then the gods with Prajapati (Brahma, the creator) as their leader went to see Lord Vishnu and Lord Shiva. They related the story of Mahishasura, their battle with the demons, and the miserable defeat that they had suffered. They related how Mahishasura had taken over the jobs of the gods—the sun, the moon, fire, wind, Yama (death), Varuna (water), and others; and had expelled those gods from their offices. Being oppressed by Mahishasura, these gods wandered on earth like mortals. Having related their tales of sorrow, they surrendered themselves to the Lord.

Lord Vishnu, the destroyer of the demon Madhu, and Lord Shiva assumed angry aspects. Their faces became red and their eyebrows were raised with anger. Then a great luminosity arose from the bodies of Lord Vishnu and Lord Shiva. This luminous essence assumed a female body and became Maha Lakshmi. The majestic form of the Goddess covered the earth and the sky. The face of the Goddess was fashioned by the radiance of Lord Shiva. The luminosity of Yama (god of death) gave form to Her black hair. The arms of Devi were shaped by the effulgence of Lord Vishnu. Thus, the luminosity of each god was blended to become the luminous figure of the Devi.

The Goddess possessed the essence of all the gods and she was the very embodiment of the energy that operated through every god. The gods were intensely delighted when they saw the exquisite form of the Goddess. The Goddess did not have any weapons. Lord Shiva gave Her his *trishul* (trident); Lord Vishnu gave his discus; Varuna gave the noose; Agni, the fire god, gave his *shakti* (spear); Vayu, the wind god, gave Her his bow and two quivers full of arrows; Indra gave Her his thunderbolt; Yama gave his rod of death; Brahma gave a *kamandalu*; the sun gave Her his myriad rays in every part of Her body; the god of the Himalayas gave Her a lion to ride upon. All the other gods and divine spirits gave Her various ornaments, wreaths of gems and flowers, and many other weapons.

Then the Devi laughed and burst forth into a terrible roar. The sound was so loud that it echoed all over the world. The oceans flooded over their shores, the earth trembled, and the gods joined in shouts of joy: "*Jai Jai* (Hail, Hail) to Devi!"

The gods and sages offered prayers to Maha Lakshmi. When Mahishasura and his army heard that tumultuous sound, they hurriedly rushed with uplifted weapons to the place from which the sound was coming. They saw that the Goddess was illumining the three worlds with her radiance. Innumerable demons rushed to fight with Devi: Chikshura, Chamara, Udagra, Karal, Uddhata, Vaskala, Tamra, Ugrasya, Ugraveerya, Vidala, Andhaka, Durdhara, Durmukha, Trinetra and Mahahanu. These were the important demon warriors, and they were all highly skilled.

A terrible battle followed between the Devi and the demons. The demons discharged their innumerable weapons. Devi hurled various spears, made use of powerful weapons, and destroyed the army of Mahishasura just as a wild fire destroys a forest.

The Destruction of Mahishasura

When the army of Mahishasura was destroyed by the Devi, the great commanders of the demons, Chamara, Udgara, and others waged a war against Devi. The atmosphere was filled with the rattling of the instruments of war, roars of the lion, and shrieks of the demon warriors. Although the war culminated in the destruction of most of the demons, Mahishasura still remained. He assumed the form of an elephant and his cries were heard in heaven and on the earth. Devi, along with Her lion, fell upon the demon, who then assumed the form of a buffalo, which was his usual form. Devi hurled a spear as the demon was trying to assume another form and killed him with Her divine sword. The remainder of the army ran away, crying for mercy.

With the destruction of Mahishasura, the world assumed a beautiful aspect. A gentle breeze began to blow. The *gandharvas* (celestial musicians) sang and the *apsaras* (celestial nymphs) danced. This is a condensed story of the manifestation of Maha Lakshmi.

Mystic Meaning

The fight between gods and demons is symbolic of the fight between the divine and demoniac forces that operate in every human being. Fear, anger, pride, lust, hatred and other vices are the demons within each human being. Fearlessness, purity, humility, cosmic love, non-violence, contentment, serenity and other virtues are the gods.

In the previous chapter, we described the destruction of Madhu and Kaitabha, symbolic of the destruction of *(mala)* gross impurities in the form of *raga* and *dwesha* (like and dislike) and their numerous ramifications.

As yet, the subtle roots of *raga* and *dwesha* have not been destroyed. Naturally an aspirant has developed a great degree of *vairagya* or dispassion. However, he must strive to overcome the subtler impurities of his heart.

Mahishasura, in the form of a buffalo, symbolizes the *vikshepa shakti* (distraction caused by the subtle desires of the unconscious) that keeps the mind agitated. Consequently the soul is unable to discover its essential nature—the Self.

Further, when *vikshepa shakti* is destroyed, the personality of the aspirant is decked with divine virtues *(daivi sampat)* such as fearlessness, contentment, purity of the heart, inner peace, cheerfulness, humility, compassion, and others. Thus, Goddess Lakshmi having destroyed the distractions of the mind confers upon an aspirant the priceless treasures of divine wealth.

Mahishasura, Chikshura, Chamara, Udagra, and others are the the forces of *rajas* (passion and restless activity). They represent *vikshepa* or distraction, *avarana* or veiling, *darpa* or conceit, fear, hypocrisy, sense-indulgence, greed, infatuation and other vices.

The description of the formation of Devi is most significant. Devi is the underlying energy of all gods, and without the Goddess, the gods have no power and cannot act. Therefore, the Goddess appeared from the bodies of all gods.

The second knot of the heart is known as *kama granthi*—the knot of desire. It causes distraction of the mind, veiling of the true vision, and perversions of one's understanding. With the destruction of Mahishasura, this *granthi* or knot is destroyed. The destruction of *rajas* in the form of Mahishasura symbolizes the realization of the *Chit* aspect of the Self (*Chit* is Consciousness). According to *tantra* or *kundalini yoga*, this *granthi* or knot is known as *Vishnu granthi* and it is located in the *Anahata Chakra* at the heart region.

As we have said, the army of Mahishasura represents the forces of *rajas* (passion) and is the cause of the externalization of the mind. With the destruction of Rajas, the subtle desires that distract the mind are destroyed. Consequently, one becomes free from attachments to worldly objects. The path is clear. The breeze of higher feeling blows gently. The ether of the heart is illumined.

No matter how far one may wander in the forest of the world-process, one is never far away from the Divine Mother One is ever enfolded in her arms.

The Glory of Maha Lakshmi

Indra and the gods were immensely pleased when they saw the destruction of the great demon, Mahishasura. They offered prayers with their hearts filled with devotion.

The gods said: "Oh Goddess, by the glory of Your power, Brahma creates this world, Vishnu is able to sustain it, and Rudra (or Shiva) destroys it. If Thy grace is withdrawn from them, they would be utterly unable to do their works. Therefore, Oh Goddess, Thou art the creator, the sustainer, and the destroyer of the world.

"Kirti (fame), Mati (understanding), Smriti (memory), Gati (path), Karuna (compassion), Daya (mercy), Shraddha (faith), Dhriti (forbearance), Vasudha (Earth Goddess), Kamala (Goddess seated on a lotus flower), Ajapa (the great mantra: Soham—I Am That), Pushti (nourishment), Kala (part or ray), Vijaya (victory), Girija (daughter of Himavan), Jaya (victory), Tushti (satisfaction), Prama (proof), Buddhi (intellect), Uma (the consort of Shiva), Ramaa (the consort of Vishnu), Vidya (knowledge), Kshama (forgiveness), Kanti (beauty), and Medha (purified intellect). These are Thy different names.

"Anyone devoid of these powers cannot perform any action anywhere in the three worlds. Oh Devi, verily thou art the power of sustenance. Without Thee, the great serpent Shesha cannot hold the world on his thousand hoods. Thou hast verily saved the gods by destroying the demons. Thou hast removed a great obstacle from the world. Thy fame has spread everywhere. Please be gracious and bless us!"

The Goddess was very pleased when She heard this prayer. She said to the gods. "Oh gods, I am pleased with all of you. Ask whatever boon you desire and it will be granted to you."

The gods said: "Oh Mother, bestow upon us unflinching devotion to your Lotus Feet. You have given us more than we deserve. You have removed our enemy. Please give us the boon that whenever someone prays to You with this prayer that we have composed, the objects of their desires, prosperity, and liberation will be granted to them."

The Goddess said: "Oh, gods, may it be so. Your wish is granted. Remember Me whenever you are in trouble. I shall remove your miseries." Thus saying, the Goddess disappeared.

Mystic Implications of the Prayer

The prayers offered by the gods explicitly describe the glory of the Goddess and Her nature. The Mother Goddess is all that is—the Truth, the essence of the entire creation. We have described how the demons Madhu and Kaitabha represented *mala* or impurities in the gross form and how they were destroyed by the Goddess through Lord Vishnu. With the destruction of *mala* (gross impurities), the *kundalini* pierced the *Manipura Chakra* and *Brahma granthi* (the knot of Brahma—characterized by *karma* or involvement in gross actions) was destroyed.

In the second stage of spiritual development, the aspirant was confronted with the subtle obstacles in the form of *Kama granthi* or knot of desire. Mahishasura, the demon presiding over *rajas*, or outgoing energy, with his various forces in the form of distractions, veiling, and subtle principles of inner vices were killed by the Goddess. Thus, the *Vishnu Granthi* (the knot of Vishnu characterized by *kama* or subtle desire) located in *Anahata Chakra* was pierced by the ascending *kundalini*.

Gods rejoiced when the Devi attained victory over Mahishasura. Victory in this stage helps one to enter into the higher planes of consciousness revealed to spiritual aspirants when the *kundalini* proceeds to the *Vishudhi Chakra* located at the throat and the *Ajna Chakra* located between the eyebrows. Mahishasura is dead. *Rajas* is no more able to externalize the mind, and one experiences great peace and tranquility.

Raja Yoga speaks of *sananda samadhi* (the *samadhi* or superconsciousness characterized by blissfulness). In this stage *sattwa* or purity abounds in the mind, and there is joy for having conquered all the disturbing elements proceeding from the lower self. The bliss of Self reflects placidly in the heart. This phase of spiritual attainment has been esoterically symbolized in the joyous state of the gods as they offer their prayers to Devi.

The positive elements in a person blossom forth with the destruction of *kama* or desire. Cheerfulness, friendliness towards all, compassion, non-violence, and many other divine virtues bloom in one's personality.

The stage of intense struggle gives rise to the advent of spiritual prosperity and calm relaxation. This is the grace of Goddess Lakshmi. After Goddess Durga has destroyed the obstacles of gross form, Goddess Lakshmi adorns the aspirant with the ornaments of divine virtues, granting him prosperity of a material as well as spiritual nature. Destruction of *kama* is the secret key to unlock the boundless treasures that lie hidden in one's soul.

Mantras for the Propitiation of Maha Lakshmi:

Om Shree Maha Lakshmyai Namah

Om Shreem Hreem Kleem Aim Kamala-Vaasinyai Swaahaa

Oh Mother Goddess Durga

*Oh Sri Kali, Oh Sri Durga
Oh Chamunda!*

*Oh Holy Mother, I see you smile
Riding on a lion, fierce and terrible,
Removing obstacles of fear;
Adversities of yesterday fade.*

*I stretch my hand to you
In the gloom that covers me.
Hide me in your thousand arms.
Protect me, destroy the demons.*

*Oh Holy Mother, light the lamp
In the temple of my dying soul.
Fill me with your compassion
In the silvery light of your love.*

*The clouds thunder as you come
With mace, conch, trident and spear,
With garland of skulls on your neck...
Now the pain and sorrow disappear.*

*Like the mighty lion truth does roar
Over the mountain you come like the sun
The darkness of grief is gone...
Joy swirls like the ocean tide.*

*The silence of night is filled
With the strange love of your beauty.
On your lion carry me away.
Oh Holy Mother, protect me.*

*Oh Sri Kali! Oh Durga! Oh Chamunda.
Om Sri Durga Jai Namah.
Oh Holy Mother, I'm your child.
Protect me, protect me,
Oh Holy Mother!*

**Song Lyrics & Music
by Swami Lalitananda**

Verse for Meditation on Maha Saraswati

ॐ घण्टाशूलहलानि शङ्खमुसले चक्रं धनुः सायकं
हस्ताब्जैर्दधतीं घनान्तविलसच्छीतांशुतुल्यप्रभाम् ।
गौरीदेहसमुद्भवां त्रिजगतामाधारभूतां महा-
पूर्वामत्र सरस्वतीमनुभजे शुम्भादिदैत्यार्दिनीम् ॥

Om. Ghantaa-shoola-halaani shankhamusale chakram dhanuh saayakam. Hastaabjairdadhateem ghanaantavilasaccheetaamshu-tulyaprabhaam. Gauree-deha-samudbhavaam trijagataam-aadhaarabhootaam mahaa — Poorvamatra saraswateemanubhaje shubhaadi-daityaardineem.

I constantly meditate on the Goddess Maha Saraswati who holds in her (eight) lotus like hands—bell, trident, plough, conch, mace, discus, bow and arrow; whose enchanting beauty is like the full moon in the autumnal sky; who is the sustainer of the three worlds, and the destroyer of Shumbha and other demons; who arose out of the body of Gauri.

Mystic Meaning

Goddess Maha Saraswati symbolizes the intuitive wisdom that destroys ignorance with its twin aspects—the sense I-ness, and mine-ness. These two aspects are represented by the two demons—Shumbha and Nishumbha.

Her bell is the revealer of spiritual insight. The trident destroys the triads—three aspects of the relative world (time, space and causation). Her plough furrows through the unconscious and fills it with divine impressions. Conch is the awakener of divine potentiality. Mace is to break down obstacles on the spiritual path. Discus is the intuitive vision that slays the demon of ignorance.

Purified *chitta* (the mind-stuff) of the enlightened Sage is the bow through which powerful thoughts are discharged like arrows for destroying the demoniac forces and promoting all that is divine.

Goddess arose out of the body of Gauri (Parvati—Lord Shiva's consort), which implies the highest manifestation of the Goddess.

Just as the waxing moon has three distinct stages—one third, two-third and full, so too, the same Goddess expressed Herself in three stages—Maha Kali, Maha Lakshmi and Maha Saraswati. The last manifestation is like the full moon shining in the cloud-less sky.

OH GODDESS LAKSHMI ABIDE IN MY HOUSE

Oh Divine Mother, here I am.
I'm not a stranger to you.
A thousand dark roads I walked
Searching in the moonlight for you.

Oh Goddess with sparkling eyes,
You appear golden like the sun.
I hear your conch calling me
Speak to me...for I worship you.

Oh look with love into my soul.
Grant me a golden intellect.
Enfold me in your fame and glory...
Oh Holy Mother, don't turn away!

Let me adore you with prayer,
Oh sweet Mother, ever tender.
Give me a red lotus of
wealth from your hand
Blow out this candle of remorse.

Oh Luminous One, give me grace!
You reap a golden harvest.
Let happiness rain upon me,
Drown me in the wave of eternity!

Like a silver star you shine.
Secretly you watch from above.
Give me a drop of heaven.
Let the pearls of wisdom fall.

Oh Divine Mother, here I am.
Cold and hungry in raging seas
In a world of time and space...
Give me the cup of immortality.

Om Sri Maha Lakshmyai Namah
I implore you, Oh Goddess Lakshmi,
Abide in my house forever more!

**Song Lyrics & Music
by Swami Lalitananda**

Manifestation of Maha Saraswati

Sage Medha continued: In ancient times two great demons, Shumbha and Nishumbha, rose to mighty power. These two brothers oppressed the three worlds, and the gods were so intensely afflicted that they sought refuge with the Goddess in the Himalayas. They offered prayers to the Goddess, singing the following hymns:

*Salutations, again and again,
salutations to that Goddess
who among all creatures is called Vishnu Maya;
prostrations and prostrations to Her!
Salutations, again and again salutations to Her
who among all beings is known as Consciousness;
to Her our prostrations be!
Salutations, again and again salutations to Her
who among all beings is known as Intellect;
to Her let our prostrations be!
Salutations, again and again salutations to Her
who among all beings is known as Hunger;
to Her let our prostrations be!
Salutations, again and again to Her
who among all beings is known as Shadow, Power,
Thirst, Forbearance, Caste, Shyness, Grace, Faith,
Beauty, Prosperity, Effort, Memory, Mercy,
Contentment, Mother, Delusion, and
Who is the Sustainer of all;
to Her let our salutations be!"*

Parvati Devi saw the gods saying their prayers as She was going to take a bath in the Ganges River. She said to them: "Whom are you worshipping, Oh gods?"

From the body of Uma Devi there ensued a radiant form—a Goddess of dazzling beauty. She spoke reverentially to Uma Devi, the consort of Lord Shiva, "Oh Devi, these gods are worshipping Me because they want My protection from the oppressions of Shumbha and Nishumbha."

Since this Goddess had risen out of the body of Uma, She was known as Kaushiki. She was in fact Maha Saraswati—the destroyer of Shumbha and Nishumbha. She is also known as Ugratara and Mahatara (more terrible and the greatest manifestation of the Devi). She told the gods: "Oh gods, be fearless. I shall verily destroy the demons."

When Goddess Saraswati emerged from Uma Devi, the latter turned black and was known as Kalika Devi or the Devi with black complexion.

Later, two servants of Shumbha and Nishumbha known as Chanda and Munda sought out the Goddess and saw Her illumining the atmosphere. They reported the presence of the Devi to their Lord, Shumbha, and his brother, Nishumbha: "Oh King, we have seen a woman in the Himalayas, and there is none equal to Her in beauty. She rides on a lion.

Oh King, since you have acquired all the excellent objects in the world, it would be befitting for you to acquire Her also." Hearing this, Shumbha ordered his messenger, Sugriva, to bring the Goddess to him by using persuasive methods.

The messenger went to meet the Devi in the Himalayas and said to Her: "Oh Devi, Shumbha is well-known for his power and valor all over the three worlds. He has sent this message to You. 'I have conquered Indra and other gods in the battlefield. I have robbed them of their possessions. I receive the offerings of the sacrifices. Since I know that You are the best jewel among women, I want You to choose either my brother or me for Your husband."

Hearing these words the Great Goddess said: "Oh messenger, all that you have said is true. I do not doubt your words. But in the days of yore I took a vow that I would only wed the person who could bring My pride down. I would only marry him who would defeat Me in battle. Please inform Shumbha and Nishumbha of My vow. Let them do whatever they think is right."

Destruction of Dhumralochana

The messenger, Sugriva, returned to Shumbha and told him what Devi had said. Shumbha was infuriated. He called Dhumralochana, the general of his army, who was a valiant hero. He said to him: "There lives a beautiful lady in the Himalayas. Please go and bring Her to me as soon as possible by adopting whatever means you deem fit. Even if She desires to fight, you should bring Her here by defeating Her."

Being thus commanded, Dhumralochana proceeded to meet Devi. Finding the radiantly beautiful Devi, he said to Her: "Oh Devi, come with me to my Lord. If You do not, I will have to take You by force. I have come with an army of sixty-thousand soldiers."

Devi said: "Oh hero, I know that the king of demons has sent you here. If you want to kill Me or force Me to go with you, what can I do? But I cannot go with you unless you fight with Me and defeat Me."

As soon as Dhumralochana heard this, he rushed to take Devi by force, but the Great Goddess simply uttered "Hum" and the demon was reduced to ashes.

Then the army pounced upon the Devi with innumerable weapons, but Her lion sprang upon them and killed many. The remaining soldiers ran away and brought the news of the destruction of Dhumralochana to King Shumbha and his brother Nishumbha.

Hearing this news, Shumbha became infuriated. He commanded Chanda and Munda: "Great heroes, go quickly to the place where that lady abides and bring Her here, dragging Her by Her hair. Take with you a vast army. If you cannot bring Her here, kill Her and then return."

Destruction of Chanda and Munda

Chanda and Munda, the attendants of Shumbha and Nishumbha, went to meet Devi with a large army. They saw the Goddess shining in her glory in the Himalayas. The demons rushed to her with uplifted arms in order to catch her. The Devi strained her eyebrows with a tinge of anger. A dark figure known as Kali came out of her eyebrows.

Kali had a garland made of human skulls and was clad in a tiger skin. She presented a terrifying aspect. She was exceedingly thin and had bloodshot eyes. She thundered with a terrific roar, and a terrible battle ensued between Her and the demons. In the end the Devi destroyed Chanda and Munda.

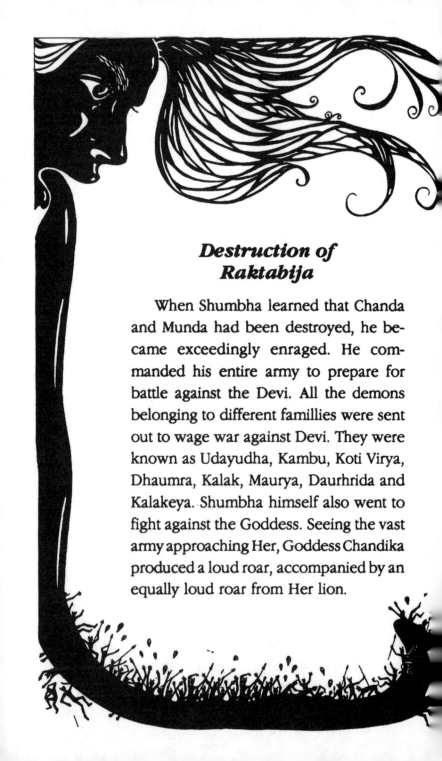

Destruction of Raktabija

When Shumbha learned that Chanda and Munda had been destroyed, he became exceedingly enraged. He commanded his entire army to prepare for battle against the Devi. All the demons belonging to different famillies were sent out to wage war against Devi. They were known as Udayudha, Kambu, Koti Virya, Dhaumra, Kalak, Maurya, Daurhrida and Kalakeya. Shumbha himself also went to fight against the Goddess. Seeing the vast army approaching Her, Goddess Chandika produced a loud roar, accompanied by an equally loud roar from Her lion.

When the demons heard this terrifying sound, they jumped upon Devi from all sides. At that time, the *shaktis* (powers) of all the gods appeared in female forms at the service of Chandika Devi. Dazzling in divine radiance and possessing special weapons, the Devis came riding on their special vehicles. Vaishnavi (the *shakti* of Vishnu) came riding on an eagle, Maheshwari (the *shakti* of Shiva) came riding on a tiger, Brahmani (the *shakti* of Brahma) came riding on a swan, Aindri (the *shakti* of Indra) came riding on an elephant, Kaumari (the *shakti* of Kartikeya) came riding on a peacock, and all the other Devis came riding on their own particular vehicles. Thus the Devis waged a terrible battle against the demons and began to destroy them, like a fierce wind that scatters dark clouds.

Then there arose from the demon army a strange and terrible demon called Raktabija, who had unimaginable powers. In his early days he had practised intense austerity, and as a result of this austerity he had received a boon from Lord Shiva: if anyone caused blood to issue forth from his body, out of every drop there would arise a demon like just him, endowed with equal valor.

The Devis hurled weapons at Raktabija and streams of blood began to flow from his different limbs. But to the shock of all, instead of being weakened by the loss of blood, the demon became more valiant, and out of every drop of his blood there emerged another demon just like him, with armor, weapons and great eagerness to fight.

In a very short time, thousands upon thousands of powerful Raktabijas crowded the earth and terrified the gods, who were witnessing the battle from their *vimanas* (aerial cars). The gods thought to themselves, "How can these countless demons ever be destroyed by the Devi and Her assistants? These demons are going to dominate the whole world. Alas! We are surely lost."

Seeing the terror in the hearts of the gods, the Goddess laughed and said to Kali (a terrible aspect of the Goddess), "O Chamunda, open your mouth wide and quickly take in all those drops of blood that fall from Raktabija." Responding to this request, Kali opened her cavernous mouth and extended her leaping tongue, drinking up all the blood as it fell.

Thus, as the Devis continued to hurl their weapons against Raktabija, Goddess Kali continued to drink his blood and devour the emergent demons. Though torrents of blood continued to gush from Raktabija, not a single drop got beyond the reach of the rolling tongue of the Devi. Soon only the original Raktabija remained, and in no time he was cut down by the sword of the Devi.

At the destruction of Raktabija, the gods rejoiced and all the Devis danced with great joy. What had seemed impossible became possible by the indescribable power of the Devi!

Mystic Meaning

Dwaita, the vision of duality, is the basis for the demons *(daityas)*. This vision is caused by ignorance. Egoism *(ahamta)* and a sense of "mine-ness" *(mamata)* are the two manifestations of ignorance.

Egoism is the demon Shumbha. Egoism is caused by lack of discrimination between the mind-stuff *(chitta)* and the Spirit *(Atman)*. Shumbha is the lord of all demons. Egoism coexists with "mine-ness;" Shumbha is ever united with his younger brother Nishumbha.

These demons are attended by a vast army of demons which are the various thought-waves arising out of an unenlightened mind. Chanda and Munda are the attendants of Shumbha and Nishumbha and they represent illusions related to action and inaction. Egoism and "mine-ness" are sustained by these two currents of mental processes: action and inaction.

Both action and inaction can be harmful or helpful. When they are directed by egoism (Shumbha), action causes *karmic* entanglements, and inaction intensifies dullness of the mind.

Dhumralochana represents *viparayaya jnana* or perverted knowledge. By the mere "hum" of Devi this perverted knowledge vanishes. Different manifestations of Devi represent the different powers of the Self—the Divine Mother at different stages of spiritual struggle.

The eight families of demons represent the eight fetters that bind the individual soul. The eight fetters are hatred, shyness (cowardliness), fear, doubt, gossip, pride of family, pride of culture, and pride of caste *(ghrina, lajja, bhaya, shanka, jugupsa, kula, sheela, and jati)*. They are respectively symbolized in these eight families of demons: Udayudha, Kambu, Kotivirya, Dhaumra, Kalaka, Dauhrida, Maurya, and Kalkeya.

By the mere utterance of "HUM" by the Devi, perverted vision disappears!

When the soul is freed from these eight fetters, it becomes united with the Divine Mother. When the ego is present, the Cosmic Mother cannot be attained. One who can win Her in a battle and become equal to Her, he alone can attain Her. The battle is *sadhana*, or the spiritual effort to control the senses and the mind. When these eight fetters are dropped, one attains Oneness with the Mother. One attains Self-realization.

Raktabija represents the impressions of *vyutthana* or the outgoing thought-waves of the mind. Due to these impressions, the mind turns towards external objects of the world and forgets the joy of *samadhi*.

An aspirant struggles hard to internalize his mind, and at times it may seem that he has overcome its outgoing tendencies. However, if a trace of that tendency still remains lurking in the depths of his unconscious, it will give rise to the same outgoing state of mind again. Then soon the mind becomes crowded by anger, hate, pride, lust, jealousy and countless other evil qualities—like countless demons emerging from the tiny drops of Raktabija's blood. What should the aspirant do? Naturally he becomes dispirited.

But as an aspirant surrenders to the Devi within him and continues to practise relfection on the teachings of the scriptures, there arise varied manifestations of the Devi (pure impressions based on divine virtues) in the battlefield of his mind to combat against the negative impressions of his unconscious. The arrows and other weapons of the Devis are the teachings of the scriptures, which continue to destroy the demoniac host of negative qualities.

The great tongue of Devi is the *brahmakara vritti*—the intuitive function of the mind that flows towards *Brahman* or the Absolute Self. An aspirant develops the vision that no matter where his mind goes, the leaping tongue of the Devi "laps" up his thought waves, and his externalized vision is given a death blow. He develops the vision that there is nothing but *Brahman* (the Absolute Self) behind every object. Thus, intuitive vision renders the outgoing movement of the mind ineffective.

Vyutthana (outgoing) impressions begin to diminish and finally become extinct. Thus, Raktabija is destroyed, paving the way to the ultimate victory over ignorance itself and the attainment of Self-realization. The destruction of the outgoing tendencies of the mind is a matter of universal rejoicing, because the internalized or intuitive mind is the source of all that is good, beautiful and sublime for the entire world.

In this stage of the story of the Devi, *kundalini* has passed from the heart center to the *Vishuddhi Chakra* or the throat center. And then from the throat center it is moving towards the *Ajna Chakra*, wherein there exists *Rudra granthi* or the knot of *avidya* (ignorance). Herein lies the castle of the demons Shumbha and Nishumbha (the source of "I-ness" and "mine-ness").

These stories of the Devi reveal facts of the spiritual battle in the deepest recesses of one's being. The demons are subtle. The power of the Goddess is penetrating and sublime.

The emergence of Kaushiki Devi or Saraswati Devi from Uma Devi symbolizes the emergence of the highest manifestation of the Goddess in the higher planes of struggle along the spiritual path. Maha Saraswati is the highest manifestation of the Goddess for destroying ignorance and, thereby, *asmita* and *mamata* (symbolized by Shumbha and Nishumbha), and for bestowing immortality and eternal Bliss.

May Goddess Saraswati be propitious to all of us and conduct us toward the supreme success in life—liberation from the cycles of birth and death!

Mantra for propitiating Saraswati Devi

Om Aim Saraswatyai Namaha

Destruction of Nishumbha

Sage Medha continues: Oh King, when Shumbha heard of the destruction of Chanda, Munda, and Raktabija, he was exceedingly angry. He and his brother Nishumbha proceeded to fight the Devi with the remaining army of demons. The demons, who were well-prepared to fight, rushed from their city like moths rushing to be consumed in the burning flame. The infuriated demons played their drums, *mridangas*, and other musical instruments to announce their arrival.

The sky became filled with so much dust and smoke that the very chariot of the sun was veiled. There were innumerable soldiers on foot, horses, elephants, camels and chariots. Seeing the vast army of demons approaching, the Mother of the world prepared Her bow and arrow. She rang a bell to rob the demons of their courage. The lion of the Goddess also let out loud roars to frighten them.

When Nishumbha saw the Goddess, he became infatuated with Her beauty. He said to the Devi: "Oh tender-limbed Devi, You are not meant for terrible battles. You are more tender than flowers. How can You wage such a terrible war?" Chandika Devi replied: "Oh deluded demon, do not say such foolish things. Either fight or run away to lower worlds."

When the demon hero Nishumbha heard this, he became very angry. He showered a torrential rain of arrows on the Devi and hurled various weapons such as spears, tridents, swords, and many other instruments of war. The battlefield took on a horrifying aspect. A river of blood flowed, and the beheaded bodies of demons danced about. There was terrific clamor and chaos on the battlefield. Many of the elephants, horses, camels and other animals had been killed and many had been severely wounded.

Proud Nishumbha wanted to kill the Devi's lion with his mace. The Mother said to Nishumbha: "Oh demon, stop! My sword is going to cut off your head. You are doomed to die." And with this, the Goddess severed his head, and the demon fell. The soldiers in the army let out a huge cry after the death of Nishumbha. They ran to Shumbha, who had returned to his palace after the death of Raktabija and related to him the story of the destruction of Nishumbha.

Destruction of Shumba

When Shumbha heard of the death of his brother, he decided to die fighting the Devi. He gathered his army and proceeded to meet Her. He saw the Devi on the mountain, shining with the essence of the beauty of the three worlds. She was endowed with all Her best qualities. Her body was adorned with the best of ornaments. Gods, *yakshas, gandharvas,* and *kinnaras* (various celestial beings) were worshipping the Devi, offering parijata flowers at Her lotus feet.

Shumbha thought: "How great and glorious is the Devi! She has just turned into Her youthful age. Her body is very tender and at the same time hard as a diamond. These two opposite qualities exist in the Goddess. What method can I adopt to win Her? If She becomes propitious to me, I shall be blessed. There is no other alternative—either I win Her over or I die." Thus thinking, Shumbha maintained his heroic gait.

He then said to the Goddess: "Oh Devi, fight with me, even though a woman should not fight. There is no doubt Your intellect has been vitiated by the ill advice of Kalika Devi. You ought to be playing on the *veena* instead of blowing conches on the battlefield. Your beautiful figure and youth do not belong on a battlefield. If You had ugly nails, long legs, black teeth, or yellow eyes like a cat, I would then have rejoiced in fighting with You."

The Divine Mother smiled at the infatuation of the demon and said: "You foolish one, do not waste your time in vain conversation. If you do not wish to fight against Me, fight with Chamunda or Kalika. I shall be a mere witness. Thus, Devi turned to Kalika and said: "Oh Kalika, do kill this demon."

Goddess Kalika was the very personification of death. She destroyed the chariot of Shumbha with Her mace. At this, Shumbha discharged a powerful mace at the heart of the Goddess. Kalika stopped his mace and took a sword in Her hand and cut off the demon's left arm. Shumbha proceeded to attack Kalika with a mace in his right hand, but the Devi cut off his feet. With only the trunk of his body left, the demon started to let out loud roars, causing terror in the hearts of the gods. Then Kalika cut his head off.

With the destruction of Shumbha, the world rejoiced and fires burned with clear flames. After worshipping the Goddess, the remaining demons went away to lower planes. The waters of all the rivers became placid and clear. A cool and fragrant breeze began to blow. The sky became free of dust and clouds. The gods and sages started to perform *yajnas* or sacrifices fearlessly. Indra and the other gods were intensely pleased. There was peace and bliss everywhere.

Mystic Meaning

As we have explained, Shumbha and Nishumbha represent *ahamta* and *mamata* (egoism and "mine-ness"), the two great obstacles in the spiritual path of an aspirant. These obstacles are removed with the severing of the *Rudra granthi* or the knot of the heart (*avidya* or ignorance) in the *Ajna Chakra*.

Egosim is born of non-discrimination between the shining Self and the *chitta*, or the mind-stuff in which the Self reflects. Due to ignorance, the soul is unable to seperate itself from the mind. In Raja Yoga this is termed as *asmita klesha*—the affliction of egoism.

This *asmita klesha* or *ahamta* ("I-ness") is destroyed by *viveka khyati* or the intuitional knowledge of the Self. When an aspirant perfects the *sananda* and *sasmita samadhis* (the *samadhis* related to the planes of Cosmic Mind) his intellect becomes intuitive. He begins to see himself as the Self separated from the mind-stuff or the *chitta*.

But in the absence of intuitional vision, the ego creates a a sense of ownership towards the *chitta* or the mind-stuff. This is expressed by one's affirmation, "The mind is mine. Therefore all that proceeds from the mind is also mine. The body, the *pranas*, the senses—all these are mine. The friends, the relatives and material possessions—all these are mine." This sense of "mine-ness" is the younger brother of Shumbha, known as Nishumbha.

OH HOLY MOTHER TOUCH ME!

Oh Holy Mother, touvh me!
It is of you I dream riding on a swan,
With snowy robe, with jasmine flowers,
On the vina you play a divine melody.
Om Aim Saraswatyai Namaha.
Om Aim Saraswatyai Namaha.

How I wonder in this world.
Without you, the rose will not bloom.
I sail in the frozen land of time.
My heart is sad, remove my folly.

The sun and stars give me no rapture.
Why are you ever hidden from my sight?
Capture me with your music of wisdom,
Oh let me look into the beauty of your eyes.

I adore you, oh Mother with shining jewel.
The illusion of desert sand conceals you.
Like the white mist of morning you disappear
Bestow upon me that freedom of the wind.

If I could only see your golden smile.
Let me keep your footprints in my heart.
I must shine like the moon in the blue skies.
Oh release me with a dewdrop of your grace!

Oh Holy Mother, touch me!
It is of you I dream riding on a swan,
With snowy robe, with jasmine flowers,
On the vina, you play a divine melody.
Om Aim Saraswatyai Namah
Om Aim Saraswatyai Namah.

Song Lyrics & Music by Swami Lalitananda

With the destruction of Chanda and Munda, the illusions related to activity and inactivity were destroyed. With the destruction of Raktabija the externalization of the mind is thwarted and the mind is made to flow towards *Brahman* (the Absolute Self). With the destruction of Nishumbha, the sense of "mine-ness" is destroyed. With the destruction of Shumbha, the sense of "I-ness," along with its source—ignorance, is destroyed.

Devi cannot be owned. Just as a doll made out of salt cannot fathom the depths of the ocean because it would dissolve in the ocean, even so Shumbha cannot own Devi because ego cannot attain Self-realization. The Self is attained when the little self is dissolved. The great "I" is attained when the little "i" is offered on the altar of intuitive knowledge.

Self-realization is not an attainment in the world of time and space because if it were like gaining an object, it would be subject to loss. Self-realization is the revelation of the Self with the destruction of ignorance and its closely related processes—*ahamta* and *mamata* (personified in Shumbha and Nishumbha).

The citadel of egoism is the *anandamaya kosha* or the bliss sheath or the causal body. In lower *samadhi* one enters into the astral or subtle body. In *sananda* and *sasmita samadhis* one enters into the causal body—into the innermost depths of the *chitta* or the mind-stuff. The *kundalini*, having pierced *Ajna Chakra*, moves on to *Sahasrara*—at the crown of the head. A yogi then enters the highest state of *samadhi*—*asamprajnata samadhi*. In this state the seeds of karmas are burnt up, and the soul discovers its identity as the Absolute Self.

The story of the Devi in this stage refers to the spiritual battle in the causal plane. When the *kundalini* pierces the *Ajna Chakra*, *viveka-khyati* or intuitive knowledge dawns upon the mind like the rising sun.

The weapons discharged by the Devi and Her numerous manifestations are the various *mantras* of the *Upanishads*. Every *mantra* of the *Upanishads* is an arrow that destroys an evil operating through one's mind. *Mahavakyas* are the great utterances of the *Vedas*: *Prajnanam Brahma*—*Brahman* is Pure Consciousness, *Tat Twam Asi*—Thou Art That. *Aham Brahmasmi*—I am *Brahman*. *Ayamatma Brahma*—This Self is *Brahman*. These four utterances constitute the *mahavakyas*, which are the mighty weapons wielded by the Devi.

When ignorance is destroyed, the bondage of the soul is released, and it attains infinite expansion. It becomes one with the Mother—one with *Brahman* (the Absolute Self). The gods abiding in the body in the form of the shining forces of the senses become delighted. The vital airs flow with perfect harmony. The mind is filled with the nectarine vision of the Self. The ocean of bliss surges and the soul is immersed in bliss forever!

For an enlightened yogi the whole world is filled with the glorious manifestations of the Divine Mother.

Glory, glory to Goddess Maha Saraswati! May She grant us unflinching devotion to Her Lotus Feet!

Look within. Be still and feel the presence of Mother. She has enfolded your soul in Her loving arms. Her loving fingers move through your thoughts, desires and feelings. Her touch courses through your pranas or vital forces, and Her smiles and frowns constitute your joys and sorrows.

Narayani Stuti
Adorations to Goddess Narayani

Sage Medha continued: After the destruction of the demons and their leader, Shumbha, the gods, with eyes beaming with joy, praised the Goddess with the following hymns:

Oh Devi, You are the remover of all the miseries of those who take refuge in You. May You be pleased, Oh Mother of the whole universe, may You be pleased. Oh ruler of the whole world, may You be pleased. You are verily the sole Governess of all beings, movable and immovable.

You are the sole support of the world. In the form of the earth You lend sustenance to all creatures. Abiding in water, You dissolve the whole world. Your strength is unfathomable!

You are Vaishnavi Shakti—the energy of Vishnu. You are of infinite strength. You are the source of the universe. You are the Supreme Maya. Oh Devi, You have deluded all the world, including all the souls. May You be pleased and may You pave the way for the liberation of all beings!

Oh Goddess, all the expressions of knowledge in the world are different manifestations of Your Own self. All the women of the world are Your own manifestations. You are pervading the whole world in the form of the Mother. How can we praise You? You are beyond words and praise!

Oh Goddess Narayani, You abide in every being in the form of intellect. You are the giver of heaven and liberation. Adorations unto You! You are the cause of the modifications that occur in the world as time passes by. You are the energy that destroys the world. You are Narayani, the embodiment of auspiciousness. Salutations to You!

You are auspiciousness unto all auspiciousness. You are the consort of Lord Shiva. You are the bestower of all objects of desire. You are the refuge of all. You are the possessor of three eyes. You are Gauri. You are Narayani. Adorations to You!

Oh Mother, You are the eternal Shakti (energy)—the cause of sustenance, creation, and dissolution of the world. You are the support of the three gunas, and You are Yourself the three gunas. Oh Narayani, adorations to You!

Oh Mother, You give refuge to those who have surrendered to You, who are devoted to You in distress. You are the remover of distress in all. You are Narayani. Adorations to You!

Oh Mother, you are seated on Your vehicle, the swan, in the form of Brahmani (Saraswati or the consort of Brahma). You are showering water by the kusha grass from Your kamandalu. You are Narayani. Salutations to You!

You manifest in the form of Maheshwari (the consort of Shiva) and You have a trident, a moon, and a snake with You. You ride on a bull!

Oh Mother, You manifest in the form of Kaumari, decked with peacock feathers. Oh Narayani, adorations to You!

Oh Mother, You are the possessor of a conch, a mace, a lotus flower, and a discus, and a great bow. You manifested in the form of the boar-god and possessed in Your hand a discus and saved the world, bringing it out of the waters on Your terrible teeth.

Oh consort of Shiva or consort of Vishnu, adorations unto You! You manifested in the form of Narasimha, which was most terrible and destroyed the demons. You are the Saviour of the three worlds. Oh Narayani, adorations unto You!"

Oh Mother, You have a crown, a thunderbolt, and a thousand eyes in the form of Indrani (Indra's consort). You destroyed the army of the demons in the form of Shivaduti. You are awe-inspiring, and You created a terrible noise.

Oh Chamunda Devi, You are terrible to look at with Your terrible teeth. You are adorned with a garland of human skulls. You are the destroyer of the demon Munda. You are Narayani, adorations unto You!

You are Lakshmi, Shyness, Great Knowledge, Faith, Nourishment, Performance of Rituals known as Swadha, Immutability, Great Darkness and Great Ignorance. Oh Narayani, adorations unto You!

Oh Mother, may Your graceful face with three eyes protect us always. Oh Katyayani, adorations unto You!

Oh Bhadra Kali, You are the destroyer of demons. You are as terrible as fire. May Your trident save us!

Oh Devi, may the sound of Your gong protect us and destroy the strength of the demons. May Your sword, bathed in the blood of demons, protect us!

Oh Mother, when You are satisfied, You remove all ailments. When You are wrathful, You destroy all the objects of desire. Having taken refuge in You, there is no misery that cannot be destroyed!

Oh Mother, You are the ruler of the universe. You are the protector of the world. The universe is Your body. You are the supporter of the universe. May You be pleased, oh Goddess! May You remove the fear of enemies from our heart!

Devi said: "Oh gods, I am the giver of boons. Ask any boon for the good of the world and I shall grant it to you. The gods said: "Oh Goddess of the whole universe, You have destroyed all our enemies. May You destroy all the afflictions of the three worlds."

The Goddess said: "In *Vaivaswata Manvantara*, Shumbha and Nishumbha will be born again. Then I shall incarnate in the house of Nanda Gopa through his wife Yashoda, and having abode in the Vindhyas I shall destroy them both (Shumbha and Nishumbha)."

"Again I shall be born to destroy a terrible demon known as Vaiprachitta. My teeth will become crimson devouring the demons. The gods and men will call me Rakta Dantaika or 'One Who has Red Teeth.'

"When the earth has been without water for one hundred years, I shall manifest for the sake of the sages, and I shall look at them with My thousand eyes. Then they will call Me Shaktakshi, or 'The Thousand-Eyed One.'

"Then I shall destroy a great demon named Durgam. The people will call me Durga Devi. Again I shall manifest in the Himalayas in a terrible form and shall protect the sages from the demons. I shall be called Bhima Devi, or the 'Terrible Goddess.' When a demon known as Arunakhya oppresses the whole world, I shall manifest for the good of the world in the form of Bhramari Devi. Thus, whenever demons oppress the gods, I shall manifest Myself and bring about the destruction of the demons."

Thus ends the hymns in adoration to the Devi.

Mystic Meaning

The Cosmic Mind is the swan of the Goddess. The water that the Goddess pours through the *kusha* straw is the Cosmic Will for the development of the seeds of karmas lying in every heart.

Triputi or the triad of seer, seen and sight, go to constitute *trishul* or the trident of Goddess Uma—the consort of Shiva. The moon represents the mind, and the *Kundalini Shakti* or the mystic energy lying coiled up in every being is the serpent. The bull is *dharma* or virtue.

Kaumari Devi, bedecked with peacock feathers, symbolizes the manifestation of spiritual power which enables the peacock of the mind to develop the multicolored plumes of good thoughts in order to devour the snakes of evil thoughts. Similarly, the different manifestations of the Goddess are different forms of consciousness in different stages of spiritual development.

The Glory of the Scripture

The Devi said: "I shall verily remove all the afflictions of one who offers prayers to me by reciting the prayers of this book. Whosoever sings or studies with devotion the sportive manifestations of Myself in the form Maha Kali (Durga) as the destroyer of Madhu and Kaitabha, or in the form of Maha Lakshmi as the destroyer of Mahishasura, and in the form of Maha Saraswati as the destroyer of Shumbha and Nishumbha, he will not come across any misfortune or affliction, nor will he face poverty, or separation from objects of desire. He will be invulnerable against enemies, royal powers, weapons, fire and water. He will never be afraid."

"Devotees should constantly study this scripture known as *Devi Mahatmya* (the Glory of the Goddess), or they should hear it recited by others. This scripture is the giver of supreme auspiciousness. Listening to my glory removes all diseases, epidemics, and afflictions. I will never forsake the home where this scripture is recited daily—I shall always abide in that home. Studying or listening to My glory is further enhanced when one performs ritual worship as well. I will accept with great pleasure whatever is offered to Me with devotion."

"I will abundantly bestow prosperity of every kind and will remove all afflictions from the devotees who worship Me and hear My glories with devotion, especially on the days that are held sacred for Devi Worship."

"If a soldier enters into a fight after he has heard My glories, he will be fearless and will attain victory. My glory shall be heard on all occasions for securing peace and harmony. When a person suffers from evil dreams, or is in intense pain, I shall destroy his troubles. I shall remove the malefic influence of the stars. I shall turn evil dreams into auspicious ones."

"Whoever worships Me with the best of offerings, flowers, incense sticks, or any kind of fragrant material; or gives food to the *brahminas*, offers oblations, and performs various rituals pertaining to My worship every day for one year, will receive the same merit that he would have gained by studying the whole book of My glory once. "

"Whoever hears of My manifestations or sings My glories, his sins will be destroyed. He will acquire health, and will be free of the influence of evil spirits. He will be free of his enemies.

"If a person thinks of Me when he is stranded in a forest, or in a foreign country, or in any place whatsoever, or caught in a forest fire, or helplessly captured by robbers, or attacked by enemies, or confronted with wild animals in the forest, or imprisoned by a cruel king, or helplessly floating in the water after a ship has capsized, or in the midst of battling armies, or in any condition of misery, he will be saved from all kinds of trouble. All the harmful forces will flee from him the moment he turns his mind to Me." Thus saying, the goddess vanished. The gods attained their former glory, and the remaining demons took shelter in the lower worlds.

Then Sage Medha said to King Suratha: "While the gods were gazing at the Goddess, She vanished from their sight. Freed from their enemies, the gods became the possessors of the sacrificial offerings."

"Oh King, that Goddess is eternal and She manifests in this world again and again to establish and maintain order. That Devi has deluded the world. That Devi is the creator of the world. When She is pleased, she confers wisdom and illumination. The same Devi assumes the form of great epidemics at the time of destruction, and She is the creator at the time of creation. She is the protector and sustainer of all—She is eternal."

"She is Lakshmi, the giver of prosperity when fortune arises, and She is aLakshmi or poverty at the time of adversity. When a person worships Her with flowers, incense, and other sacred materials and meditates upon Her, She grants health, auspiciousness, good intelligence and liberation."

Conclusion of the Story

Sage Medha said: "Oh King, I have thus described to you this great story of Devi. That Devi Who has created the world and Who is the sustainer and destroyer of the world will confer upon you the knowledge of the Self. That Devi has deluded all the beings of the world. Therefore, oh King, take refuge in that Devi. When the Devi is pleased, She confers upon Her devotee enjoyments of the world as well as release from the cycles of birth and death.

Hearing these words of the Sage, King Suratha and *vaishya* Samadhi bowed to Sage Medha and with his permission began to practise meditation upon the Devi. They resided on the banks of a river and practised austerities in order to receive the *darshana* (a glimpse) of the Goddess.

They offered the best of fruits and flowers to the figure of the Devi that they had made of sand. They offered oblations and practised the vow of fasting. They kept practising these austerities for a year.

Immensely pleased with them, the Devi appeared in Her dazzling form.

The Devi said: "Oh King, oh delight of your family, ask and you will obtain whatever you wish." Suratha asked: "Oh Devi, grant me the boon that I may recover my empire and be an unobstructed ruler as long as I live."

The wise *vaishya*, Samadhi, asked: "May I attain knowledge of the Self that destroys attachment and identification with the body, and thus may I become liberated from the world-process."

The Devi said: "Oh King, soon you will get back your kingdom and after your death you will be born through the sun-god as Savarnik Manu, and you will be an unobstructed monarch."

"Oh best among *vaishyas*, you will attain knowledge of the Self, and as the fruit of knowledge you will obtain liberation." Thus granting the boons according to the wishes of Her devotees, Devi disappeared.

Mystic Meaning

It has been explained that Suratha represents the individual soul, and the *vaishya* represents *samadhi*, or the superconscious state of mind veiled by various thought-waves.

The soul, having gained insight into the falsity and vanity of the world, turns to Medha Rishi (intuitive intellect) and is associated with Samadhi (the profound meditative process of the mind).

Sage Medha, the purified intellect, reveals to the soul the glory of the Divine Mother. The pure intellect enables the soul to discover the glorious manifestations of Divine Power as the soul journeys towards the realm of liberation.

The Cosmic Mother removes all obstacles. Gross obstacles in the form of *mala* or gross impurities of the mind are removed by the Devi in Her Maha Kali or Durga aspect. The subtle obstacles in the form of *vikshepa* or distractions of the mind are removed by the Devi in Her Maha Lakshmi aspect, and the subtlest obstacles in the form of ignorance and its ramifications are removed by the Devi in Her Maha Saraswati aspect.

She grants both *bhoga* (enjoyments in this world) and *moksha* (liberation from the cycles of birth and death). When the Goddess is pleased, She gives back to the soul its unobstructed emperorship (enlightenment) in this lifetime in the form of *jivan mukti* (liberation in life) and after death in the form of *videha mukti* (disembodied liberation).

A *jivan mukta*—one who is liberated in life—is freed from all karmic fetters and yet he continues to perform actions for the well-being of the world. When his *prarabdha karmas* (fructifying karmas) terminate, his soul merges in the Absolute. He will not return to the world of birth and death any more. The *vaishya* Samadhi (the enlightened state of mind), having revealed the nature of the Self, merges in the Absolute.

In essence, the soul caught in the world-process visits the hermitage of pure intellect, becomes the friend of Samadhi (practises concentration, meditation and *samadhi*) and learns about the unfoldment of Consciousness (the Divine Mother) through the intuitive intellect.

Ultimately, by the constant practice of *Brahmabhyasa* (constant affirmation that "I am *Brahman*") and constant devotion to the Mother, the individual soul attains liberation or *jivanmukti*. When all the karmas terminate, it attains *videha mukti* or liberation after death.

Practice of Devi Worship has two forms: *vahiranga* or the external form—such as offering of flowers, residing in seclusion, selfless service, and other disciplines—and *antaranga* or internal or direct form—practice of reflection, meditation and *samadhi*. With the help of these two methods the soul draws the grace of the Goddess or the pure Self and attains enjoyments *(bhoga)* as well as release *(moksha)*.

Without the worship of the Self (the Divine Mother) there cannot be any progress or success. *Devi Mahatmya* is the glory of the Self that abides in the heart of every individual, and when the Self is pleased, when life is lived with an understanding of the deeper laws of universal unity, the ego of a person dwindles into nothing, leaving the firmament of the heart clear of all demoniac forces. The gentle breeze of eternity blows, wafting the fragrance of immortality and bliss.

Thus ends the narration of the stories of the glorious deeds of the Devi. May the Goddess be propitious to all of us!

Turn Towards the Universal Mother

"Ekam Sat Vipra Badhudha Vadanti." Truth is one but is expressed in different ways by saints and sages of all religions. The same truth is described as the Absolute by the philosophers, as *Brahman* by the Vedantins, as the Lord or God by the devotees, as Vishnu by the *Vaisnavas*, as Shiva by the *Shaivaites*, as Shakti by the *Shaktas* (Mother worshippers), as *Arhata* by the Jainis, as Buddha by the Buddhists, as *Shunya* or the Void by the Nihilistic Buddhists, as Jesus by the Christians, as *Allah* by the Muslims. The same truth is described as Sri Rama, Sri Krishna, Ganesha, Subrahmanya, Lakshmi, Durga, Saraswati, and other manifestations of the Divine Self.

Every *Ishta Devata* (chosen deity) is an aspect of the Supreme Self. The manifestations of the Supreme Self are innumerable. Hindu culture gives the widest scope of worship—because the Supreme Being can be worshipped in countless ways.

There are two views regarding the Absolute: static and dynamic. The static aspect is called *Brahman*, manifesting as *Ishwara*, and the dynamic aspect is called *Maya* or *Shakti*, manifesting as the Devi.

Where Devi is adopted as the Supreme Deity, Brahma, Vishnu and Shiva are shown subservient to the Devi. On the other hand where Vishnu or Shiva is worshipped as the Supreme Deity, the manifestations of Devi are shown subservient to those Gods. In this context *Maya* serves the Lord: as Lakshmi, She is the consort of Vishnu; as Saraswati, She is the consort of Brahma; as Durga, She is the consort of Shiva.

Brahman and *Maya* are inseparable, like heat and fire, coolness and ice. Whether one worships the Father-aspect or the Mother-aspect, both aspects are automatically adored. The Supreme Being in fact is neither the Mother, nor the Father; for therein all mental concepts are transcended.

In the highly mystical concept of the *Devi Puja*, the Mother brings up the child (individual soul), educates him in various ways (through spiritual evolution), and finally leads him to the Father—*Brahman*—in the form of Vishnu or Shiva. The moment the soul comes before its Father, the duality terminates. Mother, Father and the soul—all become *Brahman*—the Absolute.

The concept of *Devi Puja* is indeed most enchanting and captivating. The cool surrender into the arms of Divinity in the midst of the raging battles of life and in the leaping tongues of the fires of adversities is the essence of *sadhana* or the spiritual discipline that one must adopt during *Devi Puja*.

God is to be meditated upon as the Mother during the worst conditions of one's life, and one should recline in the wide-extended arms of the Supreme Consciousness, the Mother, Who has enfolded the soul by Her varied expressions—the physical body, *pranas*, senses, mind and intellect.

Look within. Turn your gaze inward. Be still and feel the presence of Mother. It is Her energy that courses through your numerous *nadis* or mystic channels. She has enfolded your soul in Her loving arms. Her loving fingers move through your thoughts, desires and feelings. Her touch courses through your *pranas*—vital airs, and Her smiles and frowns constitute your joys and sorrows.

She is terrible in Her destructive aspect. She destroys the gross obstacles in the physical plane, the subtle obstacles in the astral plane, and the subtlest obstacles in the causal plane. She is Maha Kali.

As Lakshmi, She is the sustainer and nourisher of the constructive expressions of the soul. While Durga destroys a worn out palace, Lakshmi erects a shining mansion; where Durga removes the rocks, She produces a green meadow; where Durga performs a surgery by removing a diseased part of the body, Lakshmi performs the work of healing. Thus, this Devi, Lakshmi, is the Goddess of wealth, health, and spiritual prosperity in the form of divine qualities.

As Saraswati, She is the revealer of the grandeur of the soul. While Durga breaks down and Lakshmi heals, Saraswati reveals the potential and the latent powers of the soul. Saraswati is the Goddess of speech. She is the inspirer of fine arts, as well as any form of knowledge, whether secular or spiritual. She is the Deity presiding over the pure intellect.

The different aspects of the Divine Mother function in both the lower and the higher planes. As long as the vision of a person is limited by the senses and worldly desires, Her functions are directed towards the relative values of the world.

Operating in the lower plane of worldly values, Durga destroys worldly enemies, but, if displeased, causes manifold miseries in human life. Lakshmi bestows material wealth, but, if displeased, causes delusion, infatuation, attachment and hatred. Saraswati bestows knowledge, but, if displeased, deludes a person by filling his mind with vanity, pride, passion and restlessness. An aspirant should rise over the lower functions, recognizing the Devi in them, and invoking Her with feeling and devotion. It is then that the glorious functions of the Devi reveal themselves, leading the aspirant to the heights of spiritual glory and attainment.

The world is interwoven by the three *gunas*. The Devi is *trigunatmika*—She expresses Herself through the three *gunas*. *Tamas* is Durga, *rajas* is Lakshmi, and *sattwa* is Saraswati.

No *guna* (mode of nature) can function absolutely independently of the other two. When one *guna* predominates, the other two are subservient to the predominating *guna*. For example when *sattwa* predominates, the other two *gunas—rajas* and *tamas—* become subservient to *sattwa*.

Therefore, all the three aspects of Devi are operating in every experience and in every moment of one's life. Devi is tenderness in women, hardness in men, patience in adversities, impatience in weak-minded people. She is cruelty in the cruel, and compassion in the saints. She is desire in a worldly person and She is desirelessness in the wise. She is temptation for the aspirants; She is also the strength that overcomes temptations. She is the deluder and the enlightener.

She is supremely compassionate. Even in apparent adversities of life, the Divine intention operating through a person's life is profoundly compassionate.

In the story of the *Ramayana*, when Rama was about to be made an heir apparent, the Devi sent him to the forest to endure intense sufferings for the purpose of destroying the demoniac forces of the world. When Buddha was surrounded by all the luxuries of life, She kindled *vairagya* in him and drove him away to the forests of Gaya. When Jesus was flourishing in his divine works, She sent him to death through merciless crucifixion. The Mother's ways are indeed mysterious!

Relax in Her Divine Arms

There is great beauty in loving God as Mother as well as a profound psychological basis for this form of worship. Most human beings are raised under the tender guidance of a mother, and thus retain deep-rooted unconscious impressions of her tenderness. A child considers the mother as a refuge and there is a powerful bond of simple trust between the two. When the child grows up, however, he cannot continue to cling to his mother in the same way he once did. He now needs to turn towards the Universal Mother as his most inspiring source of support.

Simply put, if you could bring about within your consciousness the simplicity of a child in the arms of the Universal Mother—the same kind of simplicity you had when you were cradled in the arms of your biological mother—you would reach the lofty state of saintliness. If your love for the Universal Mother could become equal to or more than the love for your earthly mother, and if you could realize that the Universal Mother is always aware of your presence and that She will come to your aid, you would attain an egolessness that will lead you to Self-realization. This is the theme of Mother Worship.

Two types of devotion are mentioned in yoga: one is called *marjar-bhakti*, which is literally translated as "cattish devotion;" the other is called *markat-bhakti*, which means "monkey devotion." These have very little to do with monkeys and cats, as you will learn.

Whenever a kitten is in difficulty, it meows. The mother goes after the kitten and tenderly carries it by her teeth. Much in the same manner, when a person has attained a higher level of personality integration, he develops within himself a relaxed attitude towards life and the world. He develops an inner sense that the Divine Mother is always there, ready to help him. All that he has to do is just express his need for Divine sustenance and the Divinity will be there.

In monkey families, a baby monkey clings to its mother as she goes on jumping from one branch to another. It is the baby's role to cling to the mother. This attitude, when applied to devotion, is not so advanced because, in this instance, an aspirant is giving importance to his ego and to his own effort. He thinks that it is he who has to approach and cling to God.

All problems in one's life arise due to the ego-center. Not knowing the art of how to face your problems, you try to solve them by working through your tense ego and crowded mind. No matter how great may be your intellect, as long as ego exists with its tension those problems are simply whipped up. They are never solved.

All religions try to teach you the great mystical art of turning away from ego. The words may differ, but the goal in all religions remains the same: turning away from the ego, leaving the ego in the hands of the Divine Self, sitting relaxed with the recognition that the Divinity within you will resolve all.

This is the art that is being promoted in Mother Worship. When you consider God as Mother and inwardly have developed profound love for the *Devi*, you are able to keep the ego aside. By an ordinary intellectual process ego cannot be set aside; and that is where devotional movement has its uniqueness. When you have developed intense love for the Divine Self—a love that can be compared to the love of a child towards his mother—then by the force of that love you can set the ego aside. As you do so, your mind will be filled with increasing clarity in meeting the challenges of life.

Cool surrender into the arms of Divinity in the midst of the raging battles of life and in the leaping tongues of the fires of adversities is the attitude that one learns by adoring the Divine Mother. During our worst conditions of life, we should recline in the wide-extended arms of the Supreme Consciousness, the Mother, Who has enfolded our soul by Her varied expressions—the physical body, *pranas*, senses, mind and intellect.

The All-Compassionate Destroyer

In *Durga Saptashati,* the scripture that glorifies the *Devi*, the all-compassionate Divine Mother appears as a mighty force of destruction in the most terrible battles. How can that all-loving *Devi* be such an awesome destroyer?

The demons that appear in the colorful stories of the scripture represent the forces of darkness hidden in every human being in the form of attachment, hatred, pride, conceit, egoism, jealousy, greed, passion and the many vices that arise out of ignorance. The gods are the forces of light operating through every being in the form of love, compassion, patience, purity, renunciation, fearlessness, detachment, wisdom and the freedom from egoism and selfishness.

The scripture reminds us that life is to be viewed as a constant battle taking place within the heart of every individual, a battle in which the forces of light are contending with the forces of darkness. To fight that battle, the spirit must draw Divine energy from the Goddess to overcome the dark forces of illusion that limit the mind and bring about contraction in consciousness.

In its unique way, *Navaratri Puja* (Mother Worship) depicts the long course of spiritual evolution in the life of the *sadhaka* (spiritual aspirant) and reveals the way in which the Divine Mother leads the soul to the ultimate victory over the demoniac qualities that oppose one's spiritual efforts. The essence of the *Puja* is to enhance the forces of light, to control the senses and the mind, to overcome the desires emanating from the lower Self, and to realize the Self that shines in the cave of the heart.

To help the *sadhaka* accomplish these noble goals, *Devi*, in Her three aspects, tirelessly destroys all obstacles on his path. As Durga she destroys the gross obstacles (*mala*, or impurities) that manifest in the physical plane; as Lakshmi she destroys the subtle obstacles (*vikshepa*, or distractions) that exist in the subconscious and unconscious mind, and as Saraswati she destroys the subtlest obstacle (*avidya* or ignorance)—the mystic veil obscuring the identity of the individual soul with the Universal Divinity.

The Plan of Navaratri Puja

In the Mother Worship ceremony, the Divine Mother, or Goddess, or *Devi*, is worshipped for nine days and nights. Although the Divine Mother is One, she is adored in three aspects—Durga, Lakshmi and Saraswati.

During the first three days of Mother Worship the emphasis is given to the removal and destruction of the grosser forms of obstacles by Goddess Durga. The heart of an aspirant is tainted by the impurities of innumerable births which express themselves in the form of anger, greed, hatred, lust, pride, jealousy, etc. Such a heart is like a ramshackle old house filled with spiders, roaches, snakes and hooting owls. These invaders must be rooted out and the building cleaned up or leveled before a proper house can be constructed and occupied.

It is Goddess Durga, riding on a lion, who enters the heart of an aspirant and mercilessly slays all those impurities residing within. She levels the old complexed personality and clears the way for the construction of a healthier personality in which Divine virtues can unfold.

During the next three days of Mother Worship, the same *Devi* is worshipped—but in Her constructive aspect as Goddess Lakshmi. Seated or standing on a lotus bloom and holding lotuses in her many hands, Goddess Lakshmi symbolizes unfoldment. Goddess Lakshmi is seen as the embodiment of gentleness, harmony and goodness, and an aspirant recognizes Her Grace through circumstances of material and spiritual success and glory.

After Goddess Durga has leveled and cleaned up the dilapidated old structure of personality, a constructive process can begin. A plan is made and a foundation is laid down. Then the house is built and the gardens are landscaped. As you see more and more beauty unfold, it fills your heart with joy. This represents the stage in spiritual movement characterized by the advent of Goddess Lakshmi.

Swami Jyotirmayananda and Swami Lalitananda conducting Navaratri Puja at the ashram in Miami, Florida

Goddess Lakshmi is the sustainer and nourisher of the constructive expressions of the soul. Where Durga destroys a dilapidated ruin, Lakshmi erects a shining mansion; where Durga removes jagged rocks, Lakshmi produces a green meadow; where Durga performs a surgery by removing a diseased part of the mind, Lakshmi performs the work of healing.

Goddess Lakshmi is the Goddess of material and spiritual prosperity. She is symbolic of divine glory or *aishwarya*. This phase of spiritual movement is marked by the development of divine qualities such as compassion, dispassion, purity, renunciation, charity, universal love, unity, magnanimity of the heart, balance of mind, etc. These are rare gifts of spiritual wealth. Goddess Lakshmi brings steadiness in the *chitta* (mind) by enriching the spirit and removes *vikshepa*, or distraction, of the mind.

The last three nights of Mother Worship are devoted to the worship of Goddess Saraswati, the bestower of wisdom. After Durga destroys the old negative qualities in your personality and Lakshmi blesses your personality with positive qualities, then, finally, Saraswati—the Goddess of wisdom—comes forth to enlighten you by revealing the latent powers and potential grandeur of the soul.

Goddess Saraswati is described as having a complexion that is white like the Himalayan snows.

She shines effulgent as all her garments and brilliant ornaments emit pure, snowy light. The implication is that the Goddess abounds with *sattwa*, or purity. When *sattwa* develops in the human personality, it brightens the intellect and leads to intuitional enlightenment.

Goddess Saraswati is further compared to the jasmine flower. This lovely flower is not only white, but is also fragrant. Where there is purity there is also fragrance and luminosity. These three—purity, fragrance and luminosity—go to form the apparel and adornments of the Goddess.

She holds in her hands a musical instrument known as a veena, symbolic of harmonization of personality. The various strings in human personality must be well harmonized, for when harmonization develops, then Goddess Saraswati makes her appearance.

Goddess Saraswati is further seen to be seated on a swan, which is further symbolic of discriminative knowledge. There is an ancient legend that says that if a swan is given milk mixed with water, the swan will be able to extract the milk, leaving the water behind. Separating milk from water is a difficult task but, according to the legend, the swan is gifted with that ability.

So too, when the intellect in an aspirant becomes intuitive, it can separate truth from illusion, and this form of intellect is a vehicle for the Goddess. So, if a person has developed a pure intellect, then the Goddess will enter into his personality and will unfold her majesty through that person.

Goddess Saraswati, the Goddess of wisdom, enables you to go beyond the walls of your ego and look into a transcendent dimension. The moment you do, creative faculties begin to unfold. When your talents unfold and you begin to excel in any field of knowledge or art, then it is considered the Grace of Goddess Saraswati.

Goddess Saraswati promotes knowledge in all its forms, and knowledge is the fountain source of all that is good and wonderful in the world. True knowledge brings an expansion in your consciousness; all evils and miseries are caused by contraction of consciousness. Ultimately, Saraswati destroys ignorance and reveals the splendor of Consciousness to the aspirant. That realization of the unveiled beauty of the Supreme confers immortality.

Thus, by reflecting upon the glory of the Divine Mother during the nine nights of *Navaratri Puja*, we

APPEAR TO ME

When you walk the earth smiles
And trees bend before you.
Your crown of rubies
Touches the blue skies,
Delighting the three worlds.

Oh Goddess Lakshmi,
Shed your bounty upon me.
Appear to me.
May my dream of your beauty
Become a reality.

Om Sri Maha Lakshmyai Namaha.
From afar I see
Your bright garland of flowers.
Shower upon me your light.
Shield me from darkness.

I see you shining in the rising sun,
Your hand destroying the black karmas.
I see you playing in the old lake,
Melting the floating ego of illusion.

When the moonlight dances
On the snowy clouds,
I hear you singing of eternity.
Oh Goddess Lakshmi, gaze upon me
With your infinite beauty.
Give me health, wealth
and immortality.

**Song Lyrics & Music
by Swami Lalitananda**

see that she has innumerable manifestations as she guides Her child, the spiritual aspirant, in his or her evolution, internally as well as externally. The entire *prakriti* (nature) is Her sporting grounds and all the manifestations of the world, including the earth and the heavens, are Her glories. Her Divine ways of guiding the soul are indeed mysterious, yet always profoundly compassionate.

Through the first manifestation of the Goddess in the form of Durga, the process of demolition of old and deteriorating structures of personality is taken up, and great joy is derived through it. Through the second manifestation, that of Goddess Lakshmi, the foundation is laid down and a new structure is raised.

And through Saraswati, the third and most integral aspect of the Goddess, the gardens bloom, the trees bear fruits and, through the windows of the newly-built mansion, the soul is able to glimpse the transcendental glory of the Absolute—beyond the limited realm of time and space, beyond the misery and sorrow of this relative world. This is the climax of Devi worship—the attainment of Self-realization—and it is symbolized by the celebration of *Vijaya Dashami*, the celebration of Devi's final victory over all the demons, on the tenth day of *Navaratri Puja*.

Attainment of Spiritual Victory

Uniting with the Goddess in overcoming the demoniac forces of evil, an aspirant exercises goodness as much as possible. Even in the worst of adversities, you should not develop hatred, dislike, or morbid sentiments in your mind. Recognize that the Goddess has already ordained victory for you through the bright forces that operate within you. Even the forces of love may seem to be dull at times, but they win in the end; they are joined with the forces of intelligence and knowledge.

If the mind becomes filled with the awareness that your life is permeated by the Goddess, and the world around you is filled with the Glory of the Goddess, then a great miracle takes place—the Goddess removes the veil of illusion from the mind. Then the world is viewed in a totally different way—through an enlightened mind. The world is then an ocean of divine glory, and that is the ultimate victory in your life.

There are times when you are about to win the victory, but you suddenly turn away due to impatience. Impatience is a form of defeat, but if you are tenacious and enduring, no matter where you are placed by Divine Will, the Goddess wins the victory for you.

Day by day, your victory is in small measures. You are presented with conditions that are frustrating, that shake your sense of security, that agitate your ego and injure your feeling. Even in those conditions, if you continue to persist, to endure, to press forward with a balanced mind, you see how the Divine Goddess works miracles. As you persist, you see hatred turn into love, animosity turn into understanding, cruelty turn into compassion. These are truly victorious developments, which lead, in the course of time, to the highest victory in life: the dispelling of ignorance itself.

This is the victory which is celebrated on the tenth day of Mother Worship. It is commemorative of the mystic victory that the Goddess won on the tenth day over the demons. It was on this day that Lord Rama in the *Ramayana* worshipped the Goddess and then commenced his victorious battle against the demons. From ancient times in India this day has been considered highly auspicious, and it has been chosen as the time to begin those projects which are most important in life.

Worship the Divine Mother Every Day of Your Life

Although the nine days and nights of *Navaratri Puja* provide an intense period of reflection upon the glory of the Divine Mother, one must learn to be aware of her transforming Presence each and every day of the year. Worshiping the Devi continually through one's thoughts and actions can be a source of immense strength and joy, and it will effectively speed one's way toward the goal of life: Self-realization.

Worship of Goddess Durga

In practical terms, to worship Goddess Durga implies developing a different attitude towards things that seem destructive in life. In every function of nature, wherever you cast your eyes, you will see a beauty in destruction: a candle burns and, because of its destruction, there is luminosity; a seed sprouts and, out of its destruction, comes the young plant. If there were no destruction there would be nothing joyous in human life, for there would be no possibility for change and unfoldment.

If you hold a keen desire for a certain object or development, and if that desire is frustrated, you should not become sunk in grief. Durga can never make a mistake. If certain developments seem adverse—disease, calamity, accident, or death—you must learn to understand that there is a Divine Hand behind it. Out of pain and anguish there emerges philosophical insight. There is always a great universal plan behind everything. Even in apparent adversities of life, the Divine intention operating through a person is profoundly compassionate.

In human relationships when you are misunderstood, scolded, abused, you should not develop animosity towards the source, rather you must realize that people are nothing but puppets in the hands of the Goddess, and it is the Goddess who is testing your patience and endurance. By developing patience and endurance, you are worshipping the Goddess. That Divine Goddess does not simply need tender flowers from gardens. She needs flowers cultivated from the heart—flowers of patience, endurance, tenacity and an invincible spiritual movement that is not thwarted by anything.

An aspirant must learn to adore the Goddess in Her destructive aspect by learning to face adversities with a peaceful and balanced mind, without becoming heartbroken or angry. You must realize that, deep within, your spirit has infinite power to overcome all turmoils and all confusions.

From a still higher point of view, how can there be an adverse circumstance? Simply because the human mind cannot understand a certain situation, it labels it as negative. Reflect upon how much you owe to apparently negative situations for your strength, for your maturity, for your internal depth. And therefore, there are no negative situations. When you learn that, you are worshipping the Goddess from an advanced point of view.

So worshipping Durga, the Goddess in Her destroyer aspect, implies learning to appreciate adversity—not discarding adversity as something that should not have been, but trying to gain insight from painful circumstances. This does not mean that you willingly promote pain in your life; that is unnatural. Naturally you try to reduce pain and adversity as much as possible. But in spite of that effort, you are bound to face frustration and disillusionment because that is the law of life. As you face your difficulties, learn to grasp their Divine meaning.

The *Upanishads* say that an aspirant should adopt the attitude of austerity towards all painful conditions of life. If you have this broad concept of austerity, you do not need to practise any other austerity. Your life provides numerous occasions for austerity. And handling those adversities well is worship of Goddess Durga in a broad sense.

Appreciation of destruction also implies eagerness to destroy negative traits of your personality. Invoke the grace of the Divine Mother for the removal of inner negative qualities like anger, passion, hate, greed—the negative qualities that keep your personality in a shallow level. You must be willing to see the shallowness of these qualities, and should develop disgust towards them. If you develop disgust towards anything that degrades your personality, you are receiving the Divine Grace of Goddess Durga, and that is a great development.

Even though you may not completely control the negative traits of your personality, the mere recognition that they should not be there is a sign of Divine Grace. You should be able to detect every expression of unsaintly qualities as foreign to your personality. If that develops, you are receiving Divine Grace, and, no matter how long it takes, you are going to throw them off.

Worship of Goddess Lakshmi

In order to truly worship Goddess Lakshmi—a worship that is not just ritualistic, but one that permeates the depths of human life—the first necessity is to appreciate the constructive forces in this universe and within your own personality. Try to think of the resources that you have within you—body, mind, intellect, senses and the vast storehouse of mental energy that is locked up in your unconscious—and reflect deeply upon what you can accomplish with their help. With them an individual soul can set up a process of construction and create for himself unimaginable conditions of prosperity, glory and joy.

To truly worship Goddess Lakshmi, one must strive tirelessly to develop a fragrant garden of divine qualities in oneself, and to recognize, encourage and promote divine qualities in the world outside.

According to the scriptures, there are eight aspects of Lakshmi—*dhana* (wealth), *dhanya* (food), *dhairya* (patience), *vidya* (knowledge), *jaya* (victory), *veerya* (energy), *gaja* (the elephant, a symbol of majesty), and *saubhagya* (fortune). Thus, the worship of Lakshmi is characterized by the development of a reverent and virtuous attitude towards the Goddess in each of these eight aspects.

The first is the right attitude towards wealth and possessions. If used correctly, generously, for the good of humanity, material wealth becomes a means for the creation of selflessness and open-mindedness and for promoting goodness, kindness and compassion. On the other hand, incorrect use of wealth leads to vanity, selfishness, cruelty, miserliness, narrow-mindedness and misery. When this happens, although you may be rich in the material sense, your wealth is actually leading you to an impoverished state from a spiritual point of view.

The Eight Aspects of Goddess Lakshmi

The second consists of reverence and appreciation for the food you eat, and being thankful to the Divine Self for giving you the possibility of nourishing your body. Therefore, do not insult the food you eat, or throw it away unnecessarily, because it could have helped others.

The third is patience, which is the basis for the cultivation of all that is great and glorious in human personality.

Respect for knowledge is the fourth. Knowledge has two aspects: that which allows you to succeed in the world and that which leads to spiritual enlightenment. It is through the worship of Goddess Lakshmi that such forms of knowledge are cultivated.

Respect for the victories that you attain in life is the next important aspect of Lakshmi worship. Through victory comes inspiration, and with inspiration you can fight the battle of life more intensely. If one is not vigilant, even the smallest defeats can generate negative impressions that burden the unconscious. But every victory, no matter how small, gives you a sense of self-confidence and allows you to move on with inspiration and with ever increasing momentum.

The sixth aspect of worshipping Lakshmi consists in appreciating and developing increasing vitality, vigor, and strength, for very little can be achieved through a weak and suffering body and mind.

The seventh is the cultivation of majesty or, in other words, the cultivation of a personality which becomes a recipient of royal favor for its contributions to harmony and order within itself as well as in society.

The eighth form of worshipping Lakshmi is the cultivation of fortune in an integral sense. Fortune has two forms: perishable and imperishable. Imperishable fortune comes in the form of divine qualities, virtuous impressions and good karmas. It is characterized by a mind that is increasingly more relaxed, uncomplexed, and profoundly integrated.

Perishable fortune also needs to be cultivated, but such pursuit must be based upon *dharma*, the ethical value of life. Perishable fortune consists of money, property, harmonious relationships, friends and family, power, and recognition. This form of fortune can become a means to the cultivation of spiritual virtues as well as the promotion of knowledge. If you pursue this perishable fortune, considering it to be an end in itself, you will then be opposing the favor of Goddess Lakshmi. If you pursue objects of desire with craving and deep egoistic involvement, then even if you get those objects, they will simply denounce you. They will be there only to exert constant pressure upon you, to give you adversity, to be a source of pain and misery.

On the other hand, if you renounce the egoistic involvement and simply pursue objects because they are needed in your life for your evolution, maintaining a spirit of surrender, then you become truly prosperous. Whatever you attain will be utilized by you for your spiritual advancement.

Worshiping Goddess Lakshmi implies understanding that the wealth that comes to you is not yours—you are simply a caretaker. Utilize wealth well and the Grace of the Goddess will flow.

Whenever you are blessed with some prosperous condition, think of Lakshmi and develop humility, because the moment you become proud rather than humble, Lakshmi's Grace will be withdrawn. The wealth that could have done you great good will now turn against you.

In some parts of India, they show Goddess Lakshmi seated on an owl, implying that whoever allows wealth to rule his head becomes like an owl—he cannot see; he cannot distinguish right from wrong. On the other hand, if you utilize your prosperity for promoting spiritual values of life, the Goddess then sits on the eagle bird (Garuda) and lets you fly high to the realms of transcendence.

Worship of Goddess Saraswati

Goddess Saraswati is traditionally represented as holding in her hands a veena, a musical instrument whose beautiful tone depends on the proper tuning of its strings. Like the veena, the various strings in human personality must be well-harmonized for the beauty of the soul to unfold. One of the most important aspects, therefore, in the perpetual worship of Goddess Saraswati is for you to learn the art of harmonizing yourself day by day.

You should not disbalance your life. There must be a rhythm in all that you do. As that rhythm in life is followed—a little meditation, a little study of scriptures in good association, a little selfless service—then inspiration begins to flow through your personality. Higher impressions are generated in your unconscious that begin to unfold the intuitional potentialities hidden in the intellect.

You begin to realize that life has a definite meaning and that every day has a different message. Every day presents you with the possibility of achieving a new accomplishment and, therefore, there is no boredom in life. You become filled with energy, and all the energy in your personality is channelized for increasing spiritual understanding and wisdom. These are the highest qualities in a human personality, because there is no problem that cannot be solved by them.

Goddess Saraswati—the Goddess of Knowledge—should be worshipped day by day for the blessings of relative as well as higher knowledge. Worship Her on the relative plane by allowing your talents to unfold, by learning more and more, by making your personality more useful to humanity. Whenever you develop inspiration, a poetic ecstasy, a philosophical insight, even a new idea in business, you must realize that Goddess Saraswati has favored you. Therefore, give thanks to the Goddess and not to your ego.

On the spiritual level, seek Her help in understanding the teachings of the scriptures and developing aspiration for Self-realization. This type of knowledge is not academic knowledge, but knowledge that renders your intellect intuitive. It is knowledge that reveals your essential identity as *Brahman* (the Absolute Self). It is the knowledge that bestows liberation.

One of the most important aspects in the daily worship of Goddess Saraswati is control of speech, which is the visible manifestation of the Goddess. Words must be gentle, they must enlighten the hearts of others, they should not create disharmony and they should not injure the feelings of others. If by your speech you hurt others, if your words are misused, you are displeasing the Goddess. If you are born with a melodious voice, that melodious voice will gradually fade away; and one day there will be a croaking voice—signaling that the Goddess has withdrawn Her Grace from your speech!

In order to restrain your speech you must restrain your mind, because if you entertain ill will or resentment towards anyone, then your words will not be under your control. There will always be moods and moments when words will escape from your lips uncontrolled and you will later regret having spoken. But if, in your mental plane, you are able to control negative thoughts and develop thoughts of harmony and good will, then the words you speak will be harmonious.

Further, if you are misusing your thoughts constantly and directing ill will or even violent thoughts towards others, you will lack clarity of mind. The brilliance of reason will be withdrawn because the Goddess is displeased.

All works in this world depend upon spoken words, and spoken words are linked to one's thoughts. Those who have powerful thoughts will also have powerful words. Through positive words and thoughts, Goddess Saraswati is adored in an intensive manner. When She is properly adored, your consciousness continues to expand, until you become fully established in the realization, "I am *Brahman* (the Absolute Self)."

Thus, the message of Mother Worship is that your life should be dedicated to the Mother, not merely during the nine days of *Navaratri Puja*, but throughout all the year, day by day, moment by moment. This world is Divine. The Goddess permeates everything, within and without. You are in the arms of the Mother at all times. And therefore, live a life of joyous unfoldment and witness the victory of the Mother over all the demons that constitute the world of illusion, the world of duality, and attain the Supreme Victory in the form of Self-realization!

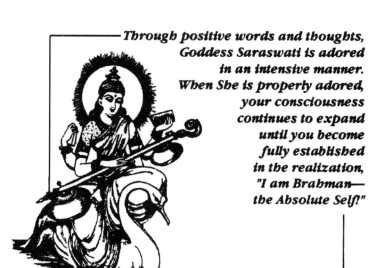

Through positive words and thoughts, Goddess Saraswati is adored in an intensive manner. When She is properly adored, your consciousness continues to expand until you become fully established in the realization, "I am Brahman—the Absolute Self!"

PRAYER TO DEVI

O Devi, tender and yet terrible,
I bow before you again and again.
Without your grace this world
Would be unbearable.
The wild jungle of fear
Would capure me.
Om Sri Durgayai Namaha.

O Devi, most gracious unto all.
I beg to touch your lotus feet.
Without thought I have
Wandered foolishly
In quest of my desires.
Forgive me for I am your child.

O Devi, more beautiful
Than the orb of the moon.
Grant me this prayer:
May I be as pure as snow.
May that longing of my soul
Find rest and peace with you.
Om Sri Durgayai Namaha.

O Devi, I am destitute.
Bestow upon me vigilance
In the dark hours of my soul.
Provide me with faith and courage.
Whenever I call, envelop me
In your thousand arms.

O Devi, protector of all.
Guide me through this storm.
The rains of misery are upon me.
Bring me back to my home
Where I may abide
With you in peace forever.
Om Sri Durgayai Namaha

**Song Lyrics & Music
By Swami Lalitananda**

Thoughts for Meditation on Each Night of Mother Worship

The Worship of Goddess Durga

First Night

• Goddess Durga is the manifestation of immense Divine force, the destroyer of all obstacles and impediments. However, even while riding on a lion and fighting demons, her face is ever lit up with a heavenly smile. Thus, in spite of her terrifying role, she is the essence of beauty and auspiciousness.

• Destruction, construction and revelation—these are the three important aspects of spiritual movement. The impurities of the mind in the form of anger, hatred, jealousy, pride and passion must be destroyed, the *shubha vasanas* (auspicious impressions) must be constructed, and the Self must be revealed in the purified mind.

• Learn to perceive the presence of the Goddess in every part of your personality. It is the Goddess that has expressed Herself in the form of intellect, mind, senses, body and all the material resources for spiritual evolution. Try to develop the awareness of being enfolded in the arms of the Mother at all times.

- In order to be a true worshipper of Goddess Durga, learn to appreciate the destructive forces that operate in nature, externally in the form of hurricanes, earthquakes, floods and other natural catastrophes, and internally in the form of frustrations, worries and anxieties, and numerous disillusionments. There is a meaning behind all these developments.

- Destruction is not as pathetic as it seems to be. Old buildings must be demolished in order to plan for new constructions. A candle must allow itself to be consumed and destroyed in order to bring forth the light that hides within its heart. A seed must allow itself to be destroyed in order to send forth the tender shoots of life that grow into a mighty tree.

- Learn to recognize the hand of the Goddess behind adverse circumstances: disease, old age, death, and conditions of sorrow and grief. Develop a spirit of austerity while confronting these conditions. Then you will be worshipping the Goddess in an effective manner.

- During conditions of adversity and misery, allow a philosophical insight to unfold within you. Pain is an eye-opener. Adversities bring forth your latent spiritual force.

If you allow yourself to be dominated by anger, hatred, greed and passion, you remain a *pashu* (an animal fettered by ropes) of karmas, and you are dragged from one embodiment to another through the spirals of the world-process. But when you allow the Goddess to help you acquire victory over these impurities, you become one with Pashu Pati—the Lord of all animals; you discover yourself to be the Absolute Self.

Second Night

• Allow the Goddess to bring about a complete transformation in your personality. Do not be content to remain the same person—subject to anger and hatred and so many negative traits.

• Let Durga fight the battles of life for you. Be an instrument in Her hands. Victory is yours. However, you must know that an easy victory is insulting to the heroic spirit in you. You must express your ingenuity, your skill, and your heroism while seeking the help of the Goddess.

• See the presence of Durga in those who shower insulting words on you. Do not develop ill will, but learn to adore the Divine Spirit which is intent on promoting the quality of forbearance in your personality. Do not develop animosity towards those who hurt you. Do not worship the Goddess for the destruction of your enemies, because your real

Let Durga fight the battles of life for you. Just be an instrument in Her Divine hands.

enemies are not outside. Worship Her for the destruction of the inner enemies in the form of ignorance, egoism, pride, passion, anger and hatred.

• With reference to "outer enemies," direct your prayers to transform them. Pray to witness the triumph of love over hate. Do not let hate become victorious in your life. The victory of hate is worse than any personal experience of defeat, because it will lead you into endless karmic involvements.

• Learn lessons from your adverse circumstances. It is the compassionate Mother who has put on the mask of adversity. Behold Her gentle, radiant face by lifting the veil of apparent illusion.

Third Night

• The Goddess is the very embodiment of the mystic process of *neti-neti* (not-this—not-this) adopted by Vedanta. She is the utter negation of the world-process. She is fully adored when the world is utterly annihilated from your consciousness through the force of wisdom

• If the world were real, how could it be annihilated? But since this world is illusory, it is annihilated by wisdom. Just as darkness flees at the invading forces of light, even so, the darkness of the world-process vanishes when the mind is filled with the light of intuition. May Goddess Durga bring about the cessation of the world-process in your consciousness.

• Develop *vairagya* or dispassion towards the objects of the world. With the axe of detachment endeavor to root out the world tree that stands firmly in the field of your *chitta* (mind-stuff). Adopt this spiritual process of destruction that leads to Self-realization.

THE WORSHIP OF GODDESS LAKSHMI

Fourth Night

• Faith, tenacity, perseverance, one-pointed devotion to the work at hand, and a resolute will—these are the secrets of attaining prosperity and success in life. When you promote these qualities, you are adoring Lakshmi, the Goddess of prosperity.

• Acts of charity, generosity, and magnanimity are very pleasing to the Goddess. On the other hand, all expressions of miserliness, mean-mindedness, and cruelty are disgusting to the Goddess.

Seek material possessions not as an end in themselves, but as a means to spiritual evolution.

Wealth becomes a burden only for one who has no spiritual aspiration in life. It becomes a means of developing increasing attachment, hatred, vanity, egoism, selfishness and all that go to constitute Alakshmi (Goddess of inauspiciousness)—the absence of prosperity from a spiritual point of view.

• Adore Lakshmi but turn away from Alakshmi (the evil spirit of poverty and adversity). Welcome the Goddess of prosperity but denounce the spirit of poverty. If you promote good qualities of your head and heart, you are welcoming the Goddess of Prosperity. But if you develop evil qualities such as anger, hatred, greed, pride, and cruelty, you are adoring the evil spirit of adversity.

• Non-covetousness is the secret of boundless prosperity. Do not be greedy for objects that belong to others. Do not misappropriate possessions of others. Be established in the virtue of *asteya*—nonstealing—and all the treasures of the world will be drawn to you like rivers flowing to the ocean.

Fifth Night

Strive to acquire divine wealth, as described in the 16th chapter of the *Gita*: fearlessness, purity of heart, devotion, wisdom, charity, control of the

By acquiring good qualities, you become like a breath of spring, bringing joy into the hearts of others.

senses, a spirit of sacrifice, the study of scriptures, austerity, straight-forwardness, non-violence, truthfulness, absence of anger, renunciation of selfishness, contentment, absence of a faultfinding nature, compassion, absence of ficklemindedness, firmness, valor, forbearance, purity of mind, humility, absence of jealousy and animosity.

- Absence of purity, unrighteousness, falsehood, lack of discrimination between right and wrong, lack of faith in the Divine Self, lust, anger, greed, pride, conceit, hypocrisy, revengeful nature, and all that are contrary to divine qualities go to constitute demoniac wealth. Strive to renounce such demoniac wealth in your personality.

- Practise *pratipaksha bhavana*—adapting your mind to the contraries. Suppose you want to remove the evil of anger from your personality. First resist anger according to your capacity. Next try to present before your mind the joyous image of love and understanding, qualities which oppose the evil quality of anger. Continue to assert, "I am abounding with love and understanding." Gradually the evil quality of anger will be sublimated into spiritual love. This process has three stages: suppression, substitution and sublimation.

- Material possessions do not go along with you after death. However, divine wealth continues to aid your spiritual evolution even after your death.

- If you abound with divine qualities, you can attain Self-realization even in this very birth. If this is accomplished, you have pleased Goddess Lakshmi in the best manner possible. Liberation is the supreme wealth which is granted by the Goddess to those who are worthy of it.

- Do not keep your mind in a state of bitterness. Do not promote *hina bhavana*—an attitude that is degrading. If you are constantly sighing about your miseries, and are fond of creating bitterness in your surroundings, you do not deserve to be blessed by Lakshmi Devi.

- On the other hand, by acquiring good qualities you become like a breath of spring, bringing joy into the hearts of others. Your presence should be inspiring to others. You should not be like a cold frost that causes the flowers of human expectations to wither away.

Sixth Night

- Do not crave for wealth and possessions. By doing so you become the worshipper of Alakshmi—the Goddess of Inauspiciousness. Deserve before you desire. If you truly deserve a certain object or attainment, it will be drawn to you like a piece of iron to a magnet.

- *Ishavasya Upanishad* gives the mystic secret of prosperity: *"Tena Tyaktena Bhunjithah Magridhah Kasyaswid Dhanam."*—"Renounce and enjoy. Do not covet anyone's wealth." Renunciation is the secret form of worshipping the Goddess of Prosperity. Renounce the sense of egoism, the sense of "mine-ness," the sense of possession. You will then live in this world with an increasing joy of inward freedom. All forms of wealth will then flow to you without causing any mental agitation.

- If you turn to any object, considering it as different from the Self, you will be rejected by that object. Such is the declaration of *Brihadaranyaka Upanishad*. Do not develop the deep-rooted erroneous notion that your happiness depends upon an object, but gain an insight into the fact that you are essentially blissful; being the Self, you are ever free of dependence on objects. Thus, if your attitude towards objects is permeated by the vision of inward freedom of the Self, you will not be deceived by them. But, if you turn to objects without the knowledge of the Self within you, you will be lingering in the world of illusions.

- Cultivate *shubha vasanas* or auspicious impressions in your unconscious mind. *Shubha vasanas* are gathered by the repeated practice of *japa* (repetition of mantra), selfless actions, meditation, reflection on the Self, and the enquiry of "Who am I?"

- Eradicate *ashubha vasanas* (inauspicious impressions) generated by selfish actions and mental impurities such as violence, hatred, greed, passion, pride and vanity.

- You are not this perishable body. You are the Emperor of emperors—you are the Divine Self. Why should you covet the wealth of the not-Self, the transient objects of the world. When you renounce this transient and illusory wealth, you are endowed with the eternal wealth of the Self.

- Become like a breeze of spring that infuses delight in the hearts of others. Do not become the fiery breath of hot summer causing pain and agony in the hearts of others. Then only will you become a perpetual worshipper of Goddess Lakshmi.

THE WORSHIP OF GODDESS SARASWATI

Seventh Night

• Destruction, construction and revelation—these are the three basic functions of the three aspects of the Goddess. In the plan of Mother Worship, the Goddess in the form of Durga causes demolition of the castles created by ignorance. Goddess Lakshmi constructs the palace of *sadhana* (spiritual discipline) and creates the gardens of divine qualities. Goddess Saraswati shines as the moon, bathing the palace and the gardens with her gentle light.

• Goddess Saraswati holds a stringed musical instrument called a *veena* in her hands. The *veena* symbolizes harmonization of the strings of one's personality. Reason, emotion, action and will are the basic strings that must be harmonized in order to allow the Divine Melody of Self-realization to manifest through your personality.

• Graciousness in speech is one of the most important forms of the worship of Goddess Saraswati, the presiding Deity of speech. Therefore, do not utter words that are false, bitter and harsh. By doing so, you offend the Goddess.

*There is no
blessing greater than
understanding and knowledge,
and no calamity greater than
misunderstanding and ignorance*

- Learn the art of honoring your own words. Words that are promised must be carried out with dignity. And since words proceed from thoughts, you must endeavor with sincerity to purify your thoughts.

- Do not entertain ill will towards anyone. It is the Goddess who is the indweller in the hearts of all living beings. Pray to the Goddess for endurance and understanding when you are insulted or hurt by the bitter speech of others. The Goddess will cause change in the hearts of even the worst type of persons. Out of the stony heart, there will emerge the crystalline stream of compassion by the Grace of the Goddess.

- Develop various talents in order to serve humanity in different ways. By doing so you will discover increasing possibilities within yourself. But if your talents are used for intensifying your selfishness and vanity, you will be like a river that terminates in a dreary desert, instead of flowing joyously to the ocean.

- Goddess Saraswati is the bestower of inspiration. By adoring Her, you overcome inertia and the sense of boredom in life. You become a highly creative person, for the Goddess plays Her *veena* through your personality with great joy.

- Pray to Goddess Saraswati for devotion and enlightenment. Pray to Her to lift the veil of illusion. Become a dynamic worshipper of Vidya Devi—the Goddess of Knowledge. But oppose *avidya* (ignorance) and its various manifestations through your personality. Let Goddess Saraswati win for you the eternal victory in life—the attainment of Self-realization.

Eighth Night

- By the Grace of Goddess Saraswati, you are drawn to *satsanga* or good association. Finding a Guru, being guided by him, and developing devotion to spiritual movement are all expressions of the Grace of Goddess Saraswati.

- Strive to develop the fourfold qualifications of a sincere aspirant: *viveka* (discrimination), *vairagya* (dispassion), *shat sampat* (the sixfold qualities of serenity, control of the senses, turning away from selfish actions, endurance, faith, and tranquility of mind), and *mumukshuttwa* (burning aspiration for Self-realization).

There are two types of knowledge or *vidya: apara* and *para*—lower and higher. Lower knowledge is meant for the practical realities in this world, as well as for the attainment of the heavenly worlds. But higher knowledge is the culmination of the knowing process, and consists in realizing the Self. Having known the Self, all is known. Pray for this highest knowledge through which all is known.

- Pray that Goddess Saraswati will destroy the demons within your mind that keep you imprisoned by ignorance. Pray for the destruction of Chanda and Munda (illusions of action and inaction—the outgoing and ingoing tendencies of the mind), of Shumbha and Nishumbha (*ahamata* and *mamata* or egoism and the sense of possession), and of Raktabija (the inclination towards the not-Self).

- Listen, reflect, and meditate upon *Brahman*. Learn the art of *Brahmabhyasa* — constant awareness of the fact that the inner essense in you is *Brahman*. This is the most exalted form of worship of the Goddess.

- Meditate upon the implication of the four Great Utterances (Mahavakyas): *Prajnanam Brahma*—Consciousness is *Brahman*; *Tat Twam Asi*—Thou art That; *Aham Brahmasmi*—I am *Brahman*; and *Ayam Atma Brahma*—This very Self is *Brahman*.

- Resolve to attain Self-realization even in this very life. In spite of possessing vast wealth and immense learning, you will not find supreme peace. Supreme peace is possible only in the state of Self-realization. Therefore, seek the Grace of the Goddess to tread the path leading to the Divine goal.

Ninth Night

• Develop the vision of the all-pervasiveness of the Goddess and adore Her as She expresses Herself in the forms of intellect, firmness, compassion, numerous forms of goodness, and also in the negative forms of craving, delusion, fear, hunger, and others.

• The sport of the world-process is sustained by numerous powers proceeding from the Goddess. Even negative qualities such as delusion, infatuation, anger, hatred, pride, passion and violence are employed in the Divine Plan. They glorify the power of goodness and present a heroic battle for spiritual aspirants.

• Though you must see the presence of the Goddess in negative qualities, you should not promote them in your personality. Anger and hate that express in others should be confronted with mental peace in a spirit of dedication to the Goddess, along with the positive qualities of understanding and love.

- If you express anger, hatred, and other negative qualities, you become a tool in the Divine Hand for demoniac expressions of life. But if you cultivate positive qualities of love, compassion, and understanding, you become a tool for expressing the Melody of Eternity; you become a channel for the Divine Forces.

- Even delusion has a Divine purpose. A person may continue to hate a neighbor for his entire life, and no amount of teaching given to him will help him to overcome his hatred. But when the spirit of the same neighbor reincarnates in his family, he directs immense love to the growing child. It is the veil of illusion that does not allow him to remember his previous animosity and his experiences of bitterness. By spreading the veil of illusion the Goddess guides numerous souls through the spirals of spiritual evolution.

- There is no blessing greater than understanding and knowledge, and there is no calamity greater than misunderstanding and ignorance. Pray to the Goddess not for material forms of knowledge but for the transcendental knowledge of the Self. Pray to the Goddess for increasing understanding and enlightenment.

- Pray for success in the practice of *karma, upasana,* and *jnana. Karma* refers to the practice of selfless service of humanity; it purifies the heart. *Upasana* implies devout meditation on the Divine Self, and it removes mental distractions. And *jnana* enables one to discover the Self through the process of spiritual enquiry.

• Resolve to attain Self-realization even in this life. Harmonize the strings of your personality by *sadhana*. Let the Goddess play the music of eternity on the *veena* of your personality.

THE GLORY OF THE GODDESS

Tenth Night

• The victory of the Goddess over the demons is the celebration of light over darkness, the victory of truth over falsehood, and the victory of immortality over death. This is stated in the Upanishadic prayer: *"Asato ma sad gamaya; Tamaso ma jyotir gamaya; Mrityor ma amritam gamayah"*—"Lead me from untruth to truth, from darkness to light, from death to immortality."

• See the Hand of the Mother behind the processes of destruction — behind adverse and frustrating circumstances. Do not give way to grief. See Her Hand behind the expressions of success and fulfillment, and do not become swollen-headed and egoistic. See Her Hand behind the glimpses of insight and inspiraton, and do not be deluded by the sense of vanity.

• *"Om Dum Durgaayai Namah"* is the mantra for invoking the grace of Goddess Durga; *"Om Shreem Mahaalakshmyai Namah"* is the mantra for pleasing Goddess Lakshmi; and *"Om Aim Saraswatyai Namah"* is the mantra for propitiating Goddess Saraswati. Recite these mantras with feeling and devotion every day of your life and feel the all-loving Mother beside you at all times.

• Pray to the Goddess who is the destroyer of all impurities, bestower of all blessings, and the Supreme Destination of all the souls that wander through the forest of the world-process. Let your life flow as a stream of prayer to the Goddess. May you attain the supreme victory in your life—Self-realization!

Prayers to Devi – The Cosmic Mother

FLOW THROUGH ME

Oh, Goddess! Withdraw this illusory veil
From before my eyes.

Flow through my tongue
So that I may praise Thy infinite glory.

Flow through my hands
So that I may serve Thee in all.

Flow through my heart
So that I may gather the clouds
Of divine feelings that rain down
The waters of cosmic love.

Flow through my chitta (mind)
So that I may remember Thee at all times.

Flow through my intellect
So that I may realize:
"I and the Mother are one!"

HOW LONG?

Thou art so near, and yet so far away.
Thou art the Thinker of my thoughts,
The Prompter of my feelings;
Thou art the Breath of my breath.

How long shall You keep a veil
Of delusive desires between Thee and me?

When will Thy exquisite beauty steal
Into My heart?

When will the gentle breeze of Thy Grace
Blow deep within my soul?

When shall this body become Thy body,
My will become Thy Will,
My soul become Thy Self?

LET ME REALIZE

Be benevolent, Oh Mother!
Ages have rolled on—Many births have I taken,
Many experiences have I gone through,
Many afflictions have I tided over;

Yet Thou hast hidden Thyself
Behind my sorrows and smiles.
Though very near to me,
Thou hast concealed Thyself in the
Names and forms of the world.
Have mercy, Oh Mother,

I cannot bear this separation
From Thee any longer!
Let me realize:
"I am one with Thee!"

Archana

The following sacred names or mantras refer to different attributes of the Goddess. Uttering each mantra, a devotee offers a flower or other sacred material to the Devi. This ritual is called *archana*:

दुर्गानामावलिः
Sacred Names of Goddess Durga

ॐ अदिशक्तये नमः। ॐ महादेव्यै॰ अम्बिकायै॰ परमेश्वर्यै॰ ईश्वर्यै॰ अनैश्वर्यै॰ योगिन्यै॰ सर्वभूतेश्वर्यै॰ जयायै॰ विजयायै॰ जयन्त्यै॰ शांभव्यै॰ शांतायै॰ शांत्यै॰ ब्राह्म्यै॰ ब्रह्मांडधारिण्यै॰ महारूपायै॰ महामायायै॰ महाश्वर्यै॰ लोकरक्षिण्यै॰ दुर्गायै॰ दुर्गपारायै॰ भक्तचिन्तामण्यै॰ मृत्यै॰ सिद्ध्यै॰ मूर्त्यै॰ सर्वसिद्धिप्रदायै॰ मन्त्रमूर्त्यै॰ महाकाल्यै॰ सर्वमूर्तिस्वरूपिण्यै॰ वेदमूर्त्यै॰ वेदभूत्यै॰ वेदान्तायै॰ व्यवहारिण्यै॰ अनघायै॰ भगवत्यै॰ रौद्रायै॰ रुद्रस्वरूपिण्यै॰ नारायण्यै॰ नारसिंह्यै॰ नागयज्ञोपवीतिन्यै॰ शङ्खचक्रगदाधारिण्यै॰ जटामुकुटशोभिन्यै॰ अप्रमाणायै॰ प्रमाणायै॰ आदिमध्यावसानायै॰ पुण्यदायै॰ पुण्योपचारिण्यै॰ पुण्यकीर्त्यै॰ स्तुतायै॰ विशालाक्ष्यै॰ गम्भीरायै॰ रूपान्वितायै॰ कालरात्र्यै॰ अनल्पसिद्ध्यै॰ कमलायै॰ पद्मवासिन्यै॰ महासरस्वत्यै॰ मनःसिद्ध्यै॰ मनोयोगिन्यै॰ मातंगिन्यै॰ चंडमुंडचारिण्यै॰ दैत्यदानववासिन्यै॰ भेषज्योतिषायै॰ परंज्योतिषायै॰ आत्मज्योतिषायै॰ सर्वज्योतिःस्वरूपिण्यै॰ सहस्रमूर्त्यै॰ शर्वाण्यै॰ सूर्यमूर्तिस्वरूपिण्यै॰ आयुर्लक्ष्म्यै॰ विद्यालक्ष्म्यै॰ सर्वलक्ष्मीप्रदायै॰ विचक्षणायै॰ क्षीरार्णववासिन्यै॰ वागीश्वर्यै॰ वाक्सिद्ध्यै॰ अज्ञानज्ञानगोचरायै॰ बलायै॰ परमकल्याण्यै॰ भानुमंडलवासिन्यै॰ अव्यक्तायै॰ व्यक्तरूपायै॰ अव्यक्तरूपायै॰ अनन्तायै॰ चन्द्रायै॰ चन्द्रमंडलवासिन्यै॰ चन्द्रमंडलमंडितायै॰ भैरव्यै॰

परमानंदायै॰ शिवायै॰ अपराजितायै॰ ज्ञानप्राप्त्यै॰ ज्ञानवत्यै॰ ज्ञानमूर्त्यै॰ कलावत्यै॰ श्मशानवासिन्यै॰ मात्रे॰ परमकल्पिन्यै॰ घोषवत्यै॰ दारिद्र्यहारिण्यै॰ शिवतेजोमुख्यै॰ विष्णुवल्लभायै॰ केशिविभूषितायै॰ कूमायै॰ महिषासुरघातिन्यै॰ सर्वरक्षायै॰ महाकाल्यै॰ ॐ महालक्ष्म्यै नमः १०८ ॥

ॐ
लक्ष्मीनामावलिः
Sacred Names of Goddess Lakshmi

ॐ प्रकृत्यै नमः विकृत्यै॰ विद्यायै॰ सर्वभूतहितप्रदायै॰ श्रद्धायै॰ विभूत्यै॰ सुरभ्यै॰ परमात्मिकायै॰ वाचे॰ पद्मालयायै॰ पद्मायै॰ शुचये॰ स्वाहायै॰ स्वधायै॰ सुधायै॰ धन्यायै॰ हिरण्मयै॰ लक्ष्म्यै॰ नित्यपुष्टायै॰ विभावर्यै॰ अदित्यै॰ दित्यै॰ दीप्तायै॰ वसुधायै॰ वसुधारिण्यै॰ कमलायै॰ कान्तायै॰ कामाक्ष्यै॰ क्रोधसंभवायै॰ अनुग्रहपरायै॰ बुध्यै॰ अनघायै॰ हरिवल्लभायै॰ अशोकायै॰ अमृतायै॰ दीप्तायै॰ लोकशोकविनाशिन्यै॰ धर्मनिलयायै॰ करुणालोकमात्रे॰ पद्मप्रियायै॰ पद्महस्तायै॰ पद्माक्ष्यै॰ पद्मसुन्दर्यै॰ पद्मोद्भवायै॰ पद्ममुख्यै॰ पद्मनाभप्रियायै॰ रमायै॰ पद्ममालाधारायै॰ देव्यै॰ पद्मिन्यै॰ पद्मगन्धिन्यै॰ पुण्यगन्धायै॰ सुप्रसन्नायै॰ प्रसादाभिमुख्यै॰ प्रभायै॰ चन्द्रवदनायै॰ चन्द्रायै॰ चन्द्रसहोदर्यै॰ चतुर्भुजायै॰ चन्द्ररूपायै॰ इन्दिरायै॰ इन्दुशीतलायै॰ आह्लादजनन्यै॰ पुष्ट्यै॰ शिवायै॰ शिवकर्यै॰ सत्यै॰ विमलायै॰ विश्वजनन्यै॰ तुष्टायै॰ दारिद्र्यनाशिन्यै॰ प्रीतिपुष्करिण्यै॰ शान्तायै॰ शुक्लमाल्याम्बरधरायै॰ श्रियै॰ भास्कर्यै॰ बिल्वनिलयायै॰ वरारोहायै॰ यशस्विन्यै॰ वसुन्धरायै॰ उदारांगायै॰ हरिण्यै॰ हेममालिन्यै॰ धनधान्यकर्यै॰ सिद्ध्यै॰ त्रैणसौम्यायै॰ शुभप्रदायै॰ नृपवेशगतानंदायै॰ वरलक्ष्म्यै॰ वसुप्रदायै॰ शुभायै॰ हिरण्यप्राकारायै॰ समुद्रतनयायै॰ जयायै॰ मंगलायै॰ देव्यै॰ विष्णुवक्षःस्थलस्थितायै॰ विष्णुपत्न्यै॰ प्रसन्नाक्ष्यै॰ नारायणसमाश्रितायै॰ दारिद्र्यध्वंसिन्यै॰ देव्यै॰

सर्वोपद्रववारिण्यै० नवदुर्गायै० महाकाल्यै० ब्रह्माविष्णुशिवात्मिकायै० त्रिकालज्ञानसंपन्नायै० ॐ भुवनेश्वर्यै नमः ॥१०८॥

ॐ
सरस्वती नामावलिः
Sacred Names of Goddess Saraswati

ॐ सरस्वत्यै नमः महाभद्रायै० महामायायै० वरप्रदायै० श्रीप्रदायै० पद्मनिलयायै० पद्माक्ष्यै० पद्मवक्त्रकायै० शिवानुजायै० पुस्तकभृते० ज्ञानमुद्रायै० रमायै० परायै० कामरूपायै० महाविद्यायै० महापातकनाशिन्यै० महाश्रयायै० मालिन्यै० महाभोगायै० महोत्साहायै० दिव्याङ्गायै० सुरवन्दितायै० महाकाल्यै० महापाशायै० महाकारायै० महांकुशायै० भीतायै० विमलायै० विश्वायै० विद्युन्मालायै० वैष्णव्यै० चन्द्रिकायै० चन्द्रवदनायै० चन्द्रलेखायै० विभूषितायै० सावित्र्यै० सुरसायै० देव्यै० दिव्यालंकारभूषितायै० वाग्देव्यै० वसुधायै० तीव्रायै० महाभद्रायै० महाबलायै० भोक्तायै० भारत्यै० भामायै० गोविन्दायै० गोमत्यै० शिवायै०जटिलायै० विन्ध्यवासिन्यै० विन्ध्याचलविराजितायै० चंडिकायै० वैष्णव्यै० ब्राह्मयै० ब्रह्मज्ञानैकसाधनायै० सौदामिन्यै० सुधामूर्त्यै० सुभदायै० सुरपूजितायै० सुवासिन्यै० सुनासायै० विनिद्रायै० पद्मलोचनायै० विद्यारूपायै० विशालाक्ष्यै० ब्रह्मजायायै० महाबलायै० त्रयीमूर्त्यै० त्रिकालज्ञायै० त्रिगुणायै० शास्त्ररूपिण्यै० शुम्भासुरप्रमथिन्यै० शुभदायै० सुरात्मिकायै० रक्तबीजनिहंत्र्यै० चामुंडायै० अंबिकायै० मुण्डकायप्रकरणायै० धूम्रलोचनमर्दिन्यै० सर्वदेवस्तुतायै० सौम्यायै० सुरासुरनमस्कृतायै० कालरात्र्यै० कलाधरायै० रूपसौभाग्यदायिन्यै० वाग्देव्यै० वरारोहायै० वाराहै० वादिनासिन्यै० चित्रांबरायै० चित्रगंधायै० चित्रमाल्याविभूषितायै० कांतायै० कामप्रदायै० वन्द्यायै० विद्याधरसुपूजितायै० श्वेताननायै० नीलभुजायै० चतुर्वर्गफलप्रदायै० चतुराननसाम्राज्यै० रक्तमध्यायै० ब्रह्माविष्णुशिवात्मिकायै नमः १०८॥

Selections from Devi Sukta

ॐ

देवी सूक्तम्

नमो देव्यै महादेव्यै शिवायै सततं नमः ।
नमः प्रकृत्यै भद्रायै नियताः प्रणतास्मताम् ॥

Namo Devyai mahadevyai shivaayai satatam namah.
Namah prakrityai bhadraayai niyataah pranatasmataam.

Adorations to the Devi, adorations to the Great Devi, our constant adorations to Her who is ever auspicious, who is the material cause of the universe, who is the embodiment of goodness and gentleness.

रौद्रायै नमो नित्यायै गौर्यै धात्र्यै नमो नमः ।
ज्योत्स्नायै चेन्दुरूपिण्यै सुखायै सततं नमः ॥

Raudrayai namo nityaayai gauryai dhaatryai namo namah
Jyotsnaayai chenduroopinyai sukhaayai satatam namah.

Adorations always to Her who is terrible, to Her who is eternal; who is known as Gauri (Shiva's consort) and Dhatri (the nourisher of the universe). Adorations always to Her who is lustrous as the moonlight as well as who is of the form of the moon; who is the very embodiment of Bliss.

या देवी सर्वभूतेषु विष्णुमायेति शब्दिता।
नमस्तस्यै नमस्तस्यै नमस्तस्यै नमो नमः॥

*Yaa devi sarva-bhooteshu vishnu-maayeti shabditaa
Namastasyai namastasyai namastasyai namo namah.*

Salutations to the Devi, who is known as Lord Vishnu's Maya operating through all beings. Again and again adorations to Her!

या देवी सर्वभूतेषु चेतनेत्यभिधीयते।
नमस्तस्यै नमस्तस्यै नमस्तस्यै नमो नमः॥

*Yaa devee sarvabhooteshu chetanetyabhidheeyate
Namastasyai namastasyai namastasyai namo namah.*

Salutations to the Devi, who is known as Consciousness in all beings. Again and again adorations to Her!

या देवी सर्वभूतेषु बुद्धिरूपेणसंस्थिता।
नमस्तस्यै नमस्तस्यै नमस्तस्यै नमो नमः॥

*Yaa devee sarvabhooteshu buddhi roopena samsthitaa
Namastasyai namastasyai namastasyai namo namah.*

Salutations to the Devi, who abides as Intellect in all beings. Adorations, again and again adorations to Her!

या देवी सर्वभूतेषु लक्ष्मीरूपेणसंस्थिता।
नमस्तस्यै नमस्तस्यै नमस्तस्यै नमो नमः॥

*Yaa devee sarvabhooteshu Lakshmee roopena samsthitaa
Namastasyai namastasyai namastasyai namo namah.*

Salutations to the Devi, who abides as Lakshmi--the Goddess of Prosperity in all beings. Adorations, again and again adorations to Her!

Arati

The Waving of Light Ceremony

One of the most graceful and significant acts of worship among the Hindus is *arati* or the waving of light. This worship is performed by burning camphor on a plate and then moving the plate in a circular motion in front of the statue or the picture of the Deity. While the light produced from the burning camphor continues burning, mantras are chanted, invoking the Divinity in His or Her various aspects.

When the chanting of the mantras is over, the plate with the burning flame is passed around so that every devotee may pay reverence to the sacred flame

by gracefuly extending the palms of his hands towards the flame and then placing the palms over his eyes. At the end of *arati* a prayer is conducted for universal peace and auspiciousness for all. *Prasad* or sacred food is then distributed among the devotees.

Light is the symbol of the Self. The Self is the Light of all lights. Paying reverence to the light and offering it to the Divinity is a symbolic act for propitiating the Light of Knowledge that removes the veil of ignorance.

When the devotee brings his palms over his eyes, he is expressing his devout prayer: "Oh, Light of the Supreme, may You bestow upon me the vision of the Self. May my intellect be illumined by the Light of intuition, and just as camphor melts in fire, even so, may my ego melt in *Brahman* or the Absolute."

The burning of incense sticks symbolizes the fragrance of a life that has been lit up by intuition. When the heart is free from impurities, and life is kindled with divine aspiration, a beautiful aroma pervades every action of a person. It is the aroma of spiritual vision. Fragrance is hidden in the incense stick and emanates when it has been burned; even so, divine virtues such as contentment, humility, and compassion are hidden in every being and they unfold when the ego is burned by the fire of Divine love.

Prasad or sacred food is distributed at the end of all religious ceremonies. The sacred food is charged with divine vibrations, and becomes a medium for receiving Divine grace. The vibrations of mantras, blended with the faith of the devotee, lend an amazing mystical power to the *prasad*. It can heal the ailments of the body and the mind.

Kumkum, a red powder, is the *prasad* of the Devi. It is applied between the eyebrows, the location of the mystic center known as the *Ajna Chakra*, or the eye of intuition. When *kumkum* is applied, this spiritual center is as if blessed by the Devi.

Vibhuti, or ashes, is the *prasad* of Lord Shiva and is applied on the forehead. Wearing *vibhuti* is symbolic of aspiring to reduce all karmas or actions into ashes by Divine grace.

Arati

Jaya Jaya Aarati Vighna Vinaayaka

Vighna Vinaayaka Sri Ganesha

Jaya Jaya Aarati Subrahmanya

Subrahmanya Kaartikeya

Jaya Jaya Aarati Venugopaala,

Venugopalaa Venulola

Paap Viduraa Navaneeta Choraa

Jaya Jaya Aarati Venkata Ramanaa

Venkata Ramanaa Shankata Haranaa

Seeta Rama Raadhe Shyaamaa

Jaya Jaya Aarati Gauri Manohar

Gauri Manohar Bhavaani Shankara

Samba Sadaashiva Umaa Maheshwara

Jaya Jaya Aarati Raaja Raajeshwari

Raaja Raajeshwari Tripura Sundaree

Mahaa Lakshmi Mahaa Saraswati

Mahaa Kalai Mahaa Shakti

Jaya Jaya Aarati Aanjaneya

Aanjaneya Hanoomanta

Jaya Jaya Aarati Dattaatreya

Dattaareya, Trimoorti Avataara

Jaya Jaya Aarati Shanaishwaraaya

Shanaishwaraaya Bhaaskaraaya

Jaya Jaya Aarati Sadguru Naatha,

Sadguru Naatha Shivaananda

Jaya Jaya Aarati Vighna Vinaayaka

Na Tatra Suryo Bhaati, Na Chandra Taarakam

Nemaa Vidyuto Bhaanti Kutoyam Agnih

Tameva Bhaantam Anubhaati Sarvam

Tasya Bhaashaa Sarvamidam Vibhaati

The English Meaning of Arati

Glory, glory to Ganesha,
The remover of all obstacles,

Glory, glory to Subrahmanya,
The Son of Lord Shiva—Kartikeya,

Glory, glory to the Flute-player,
Glory, glory to Lord Krishna.
Glory, glory to the Flute Player
The Destroyer of sins, and Stealer of butter.

Glory, glory to Lord Vishnu
Destroyer of all afflictions;
Sita and Rama, Radha and Shyama.

Glory, glory to Mother Gauri,
Glory to Bhavani and Shankara,

Glory to Lord Shiva with his consort Uma,

Glory to the Great Goddess
The Beauty of the three worlds,
Glory to Maha Lakshami—Giver of prosperity,
Glory to Maha Saraswati,
Glory to Maha Kali and to Maha Shakti

Glory, glory to Lord Hanuman,
Son of Anjana Devi

Glory, glory to Dattatreya
The incarnation of the three Divinities,

Glory, glory to the Shanaishwara,
the Deity Of Saturn and to the Sun-God, glory,

Glory to the Guru, Swami Sivananda

Glory, glory to Ganesha,
The destroyer of obstacles!

Neither the sun nor the moon
nor the stars shine there
Nor does shine lightning, much less this fire;
When He shines all the luminaries
shine after Him
By His Light all these are illumined!

O GODDESS LAKSHMI, SMILE UPON ME

*O Goddess Lakshmi,
Smile upon me.
Cast Thy sidelong glance unto me.
Awaken me from
My long, long dream.*

*In the garden of my life
Let every leaf that
Blows in the wind
Turn into radiant gold.
Let every flower
Become a perfect gem
That lights up my lonely heart.*

*O Goddess Lakshmi,
Grant me the vision of
Thy lotus feet
On the sands of eternity.*

*Inspire me to climb the
Mystic mountain.
Let my soul become a
Cascading stream of your grace,
Carrying a love unkown to
All who walk on earth.
O Goddess Lakshmi,
Smile upon me.*

Song lyrics & music by Swami Lalitananda

Following the *arati*, the following mantras may be recited:

Chants for Auspiciousness

*Om Swasti Prajaabhyaha Paripaalayantam
Nyayenamaargena Meheem Maheeshaaha
Go Braahmanebhyaha Shubhamastu Nityam
Lokaah Samastah Sukhino Bhavantu
Kale Varshantu Parjanyah
Prithvee Shashya Shaalini
Deshoyam Kshobharahito
Braahmanah Santu Nirbhayaah
Ashubhaani Niraacheste
Tanoti Shubha Santatim
Smritimaatrena Yat Punsaam
Brahma Tan Mangalam Viduh
Ati Kalyaana Rupatwaat
Nitya Kalyaana Samshrayaat
Smartirnaam Varadatwaatcha
Brahma Tanmangalam Viduh
Om Karascha atha Shabdascha
Dwavetau Brahmanaa Puraa
Kanthan Bhitwaa Viniryatau
Tasmaanmangalikaavubhau
Atha Om, Atha Om, Atha Om
Mangalam Me Asmaad Gurunaam
Mangalam Me Astu
Sarveshaam Mangalam Bhavatu*

Om Sarveshaam Swastir Bhavatu
Sarveshaam Shaantir Bhavatu
Sarveshaam Poornam Bhavatu
Sarveshaam Mangalam Bhavatu
Sarve Bhavantu Sukhinah
Sarve Santu Niraamayaah
Sarve Bhadraani Pashyantu
Ma Kaschit Dukh Bhaag Bhavet
Asato Maa Sad Gamaya
Tamaso Maa Jyotir Gamaya
Mrityor Maa Amritam Gamaya.

Meaning of the Chants for Auspiciousness

May the kings rule the earth justly and
Protect the people, giving them justice!
May good befall cows (all living beings)
and *brahmins*!
May the people of the whole world be happy!
May rains fall at the proper time!
May the earth become very fertile!
May the country be free from famine!
May the *brahminas* become fearless
and rest peacefully!

By merely thinking of *Brahman*,
One destroys all that is inauspicious.
That *Brahman* bestows a continuous stream of joy
And happiness in all.
He is the very personification
Of auspiciousness Itself!
The knowers of *Brahman* regard *Brahman* as
All auspiciousness
Because He is the embodiment of auspiciousness
Also because He gratifies the desires
Of those who think of Him.
Om and *Atha* were the first utterances given
By Brahma (at the time of creation);
Therefore, these two words coming
From Brahma's lips are very auspicious.
Atha Om, Atha Om, Atha Om—
Let this be our chant.
Let auspiciousness be unto our teachers,
And let auspiciousness be unto me.
Let auspiciousness be unto one and all!
May prosperity be unto all,
May peace be unto all,
May fullness be unto all,
May auspiciousness be unto all!
May all become happy,
May all be healthy and free from diseases,
May all see good only.
Let no one undergo suffering!

Lead me from untruth to truth,
Lead me from darkness to light,
Lead me from death to immortality.

Peace Chant

*Om Poornamadah, Poornamidam
Poornaat Poornamudachyate
Poornasya Purnamaadaaya
Purnamevaavashisyate
Om Shaantih, Shaantih, Shaantih*

Meaning of the Peace Chant

That (Absolute) is full. This (world, being a manifestation of the Absolute) is full. When this (world-process) is taken away (by transcending it through Self-realization), what remains is full (the Absolute). Om Peace, Peace, Peace!

(This is a mystic verse conveying the fullness of the Absolute and Its unity with the world.)

O GODDESS SARASWATI

In the moonlight I hear your vina,
O Goddess of supreme beauty.
Your garland of sweet flowers
Captures my longing soul.
I bow in deep devotion.

Grant me a golden intellect.
May my mind be ever pure.
Om Aim Saraswatyai Namaha.

O Goddess, your eyes shine
Like the dew drops
On the morning rose.
I meditate on
Your dazzling form,
Seated on the heavenly swan.
Bestow upon me the
Divine wisdom of
Thy infinite Self.

Song Lyrics & Music by Swami Lalitananda

Meditation on the Mother As Energy

The following exercises lead you into meditation upon energy in its various forms from gross to subtle: from physical energy, (referred to as *kriya shakti*), to psychic energy (referred to as *iccha shakti*), to the subtlest energy of Wisdom (referred to as *jnana shakti*). Each of these forms of energy is associated with an aspect of the Divine Self as Mother: Goddess Durga, Goddess Lakshmi, or Goddess Saraswati.

Begin your focus on *kriya shakti* by viewing the vast physical world as a surging ocean of energy. Feel that you are an integral part of this great creation, and you are totally permeated by its universal energy. The energy that rages in storms and winds and lightening, and unfolds gently in tender flowers and leaves—that same energy pulsates in your heart, flows in your veins, sustains every living cell within your body.

Focus your mind at the navel center, and feel that *kundalini* is awake at that center. Mentally visualize Goddess Durga, who represents *kriya shakti*, the energy that operates in the physical world. As you mentally repeat the mantra *Om Dum Durgayai Namah*, feel you are one with universal energy. Let that increasing awareness of unity with *kriya shakti* remove all sense of physical weakness from your mind.

Turn your attention to the subtler and more pervasive form of energy—*icha shakti*—the psychic energy behind your thoughts and desires. Faster than light, thoughts travel in all directions as vibrations in the mental atmosphere. Every thought that you send out is a vibration which never perishes. It goes on vibrating in every particle of the universe.

Think of the tremendous power of thoughts. They can work unimaginable wonders of healing or destruction. They control your life and mold your character. Thoughts of great men continue to shape the destiny of humanity for centuries and centuries. That psychic energy that surges through the mental universe is an inherent part of yourself.

Focus your mind at the heart center and feel that *kundalini* is awake at that center. Mentally visualize Goddess Lakshmi, who represents *iccha shakti*, the universal mental energy. As you mentally repeat the mantra *Om Sri Mahalakshmyai Namah*, feel oneness with that universal mental energy.

Inwardly assert, "My mind is filled with dynamic energy. My thoughts are powerful. My will is strong. The power hidden in my mind is beyond all imagination." As this awareness grows and your mind captures even a glimpse of universal mental energy, it has no room for thoughts of worry, anxiety or negativity of any kind.

Shift your attention to the subtlest form of energy—*jnana shakti*—the energy of wisdom, the energy of the intuitive mind. Think of the Divine intelligence that permeates every atom in the entire creation. The Self, as the embodiment of knowledge, is the essence of every soul. The climax of all human knowledge is the realization,"I am That." Nothing in this world is more powerful than the power of knowledge. It shatters the illusion of the world-process with a single blow.

Focus your mind on the *Ajna Chakra*, and by mental suggestion feel that *kundalini* is radiating from that center. Mentally visualize Goddess Saraswati, who represents *jnana shakti*– the energy of Divine wisdom, of Knowledge Absolute. As you mentally repeat *Om Aim Saraswatyai Namah*, feel that the Giver of Knowledge is endowing you with the blazing light of intuition. Feel that just as light removes darkness, that effulgent intuitive light is removing ignorance forever.

O DEVI DURGA

*Oh gracious Mother,
In the dark of the night,
When I cry with pain,
I think of you
And you give me strength.*

*O Goddess Durga, protect me
From the dark clouds of sorrow.
May I be pure,
pure like the shining snow.*

*The wild ghosts of yesterday
Haunt me with memories.
Now I surrender to you.
May my delusion be gone.*

*O Goddess Durga, protect me
From the dark clouds of sorrow.
May I be pure,
Pure like the shining snow.*

*Oh gracious Mother,
By You the universe is created.
By You the universe is protected
And unto You the universe dissolves.
May You shower goodness up on all.*

*O Goddess Durga, protect me
From the dark clouds of sorrow.
May I be pure,
Pure like the shining snow.
Oh gracious Mother,
With Your swift sword
Remove my old maladies
And bring me health,
Wealth, and immortality.*

Om Sri Durgayai Namaha

**Song lyrics & Music
by Swami Lalitananda**

The Mysterious Ways of Maya

—A Parable Adapted from Devi Bhagavata—

Once upon a time, Sage Narada went to Vaikuntha, where Lord Vishnu dwells. When the Sage entered, Vishnu welcomed him warmly, but, to Narada's surprise, Goddess Lakshmi put a veil before her face and turned away from him. Dismayed and perplexed, Narada asked Lord Vishnu, "Why did Goddess turned away from me—I who am so pure minded, a person of great austerity?" Lord Vishnu replied, "You never know the subtle delusion that operates through one's unconscious. *Maya* is difficult to understand, Oh, Narada."

Narada then pleaded before Lord Vishnu, "Oh Lord, show me your *Maya*. Let me understand what it is." Lord Vishnu said, "Very well. Soon I shall explain it to you, but let us go for a ride in the heavenly world first."

He then invoked the presence of the great bird Garuda, who swiftly appeared and carried them through the blue sky until they came to a beautiful and enchanting place, abounding with crystal-clear streams, and trees laden with blossoms.

There Lord Vishnu said, "Let us have a plunge in this wonderful stream and then rest," said Lord Vishnu. "You go first, Narada." "Yes my Lord," said Narada, and he handed Lord Vishnu his veena, a stringed instrument he carried with him wherever he went.

Then Narada entered the lake. The moment he put his head under the water, his whole personality and his body changed, transformed by *Maya*. When he emerged, there was no Lord Vishnu, no Narada—there was only a beautiful lady. And that lady, well-dressed, and bewildered by her presence in the lake, did not know where she came from or who she was.

As she stood there in confusion, a king, Taladhwaja, passed by with his royal retinue as they were engaged in a hunting expedition through the forest. Suddenly he saw the lady and was immediately enchanted by her beauty. "Who are you?" said Taladhwaja. The lady replied, "Oh king, I do not know." The king proposed that she become his queen, and the lady agreed because she did not have any protector.

Thus the lady became the supermost queen of the great king and the king loved her the most of all his wives. Time passed, and the lady, whose name became Saubhagya Sundari, remained completely unaware that she was essentially Narada. In the course of time she bore twelve sons, one after the other. As these sons were growing up, the lady, who was really Narada, was constantly involved in solving the problems in her large family—tending to quarrels, celebrating birthdays, caring for sickness, delighting in their attainments.

In the course of time, a powerful enemy attacked the kingdom. In order to meet that enemy and his vast army, the king along with his sons, went out to battle. And a fierce battle it was, resulting in the death of all the royal sons of Saubhagya Sundari. The king, however, although badly defeated, escaped death.

When the queen came to know of the defeat of her husband and the destruction of her family, she experienced intense grief. She rushed to the battlefield to see the bodies of her sons, who she loved so dearly, and there she grieved even more intensely.

During that time, Lord Vishnu, in the form of an old ascetic, appeared before her saying, "Oh lady, why do you grieve? This is the nature of things. All that is born must die. Further, by grieving, you do not help the departed souls. You should rather enter the water of this stream and perform rituals and prayers for the peace of those souls."

The queen plunged into the stream and as she emerged she found herself again transformed into Narada. Lord Vishnu was there smiling, holding the veena of the Sage in his hand. He said, "Oh Sage, you are taking much time." And Narada realized then that all his experiences had been the mysterious workings of *Maya*.

Mystic Meaning

Essentially, we are all Saint Narada; we are all Divine. But when we enter the stream of *avidya* or ignorance, the enchanting stream of the conditioned mind, we are transformed into a *jiva*, or individualized soul.

As an individualized soul, you become wedded to your ego and spend your years struggling to find solutions for problems in the world of time and space—where there are no permanent solutions for anything.

Absorbed in your family and material possessions, you find it natural to think that these are the only things of importance. As a result, you live only for these perishable things, not realizing that you are essentially the Spirit.

It is only through spiritual association, study of scriptures and meditation that you develop *vairagya* (dispassion) and realize that everything will pass away. Nothing that you depend upon can be dependable all the time. You gain insight into the subtle and mysterious workings of *Maya*, and strive to learn the art of mystic awakening.

Thus, you are led to another kind of stream: *Jnana Ganga*, or the stream of wisdom and knowledge. The moment you enter into that stream, you emerge in your own essential form—as if awakened from the sway of Lord Vishnu's *Maya*, and you find the Divine Self smiling before you. You cast off the illusion of jivahood—the sense of individuality, and emerge as *Brahman*. All your miseries and sorrows, all the experiences of countless embodiments, fade from your view—like the experiences of a long dream; and you realize, "I am *Brahman*—the Absolute Self."

The great message of *Vijaya Dashami*—the Day of Victory which constitutes the tenth day of Mother worship—is that you have a choice: you can either keep ducking into the stream of ignorance and move from illusion to illusion, or you can enter the stream of knowledge and recapture your essential identity as the Divine Self. One who makes the right choice emerges victorious and attains the goal of life.

May the Divine Mother bless you with insight, understanding, and enlightenment.

The Rise and Fall of the Ego

(A mystical story from the *Devi Bhagavata* that speaks of the glory of Goddess)

Once there was a great and powerful king in ancient India named Nahusha. During his reign he performed various sacrifices and righteous acts. Because of his meritorious deeds, his ability to enjoy heavenly delights was heightened.

According to the story, Indra, the king of gods, had to go into seclusion for some time and stay away from his normal duties. Immediately there arose the question of who would rule the heavenly world in Indra's absence. The gods and sages therefore convened to choose a successor. In reviewing the possible candidates, they found that King Nahusha of the mortal world had attained great spiritual qualities and undoubtedly deserved to be ruler of Heaven; so they proposed that Nahusha succeed Indra as ruler.

Immediately a messenger was dispatched to report their decision to King Nahusha. He was told that he was promoted to the heavenly world and that he would become the new Indra—ruler of the gods. Nahusha was highly pleased to hear this news and he entered the heavenly world and began his rulership.

But such exaltation, instead of making him humbler, made him swollen-headed. Formerly he had been a righteous person, but actually his "righteousness" had not been very profound; ego still dominated his mind to a great extent. Because of this he gradually developed intense pride in his position in the heavenly world. The gods and sages were not pleased with the changes in Nahusha, but since they had chosen him for this position, they allowed him to have his way.

Soon, however, Nahusha's pride grew even more and he began to covet Indra's wife, Indrani Shachi. His mind was constantly obsessed with the thought, "Why shouldn't Shachi become my wife? Just think of the glory and prestige she would bring me."

Presently news was sent to Shachi that she should come and accept Nahusha as her husband. When Shachi was brought before him, Nahusha said to her, "You shall accept me as your husband, and both of us then will enjoy the heavenly glory. Think no more of your husband who is dead and gone. Even if he is alive he may as well be dead, because he is no longer ruling the heavenly realm."

Shachi tried to persuade Nahusha not to insist on her becoming his wife, but he was adamant and wouldn't hear of it. The more she pleaded the angrier he got. Seeing Nahusha's anger, even the gods and sages were afraid. They did not know what to do about his terrible ego, or how to divest him of the power they had invested in him.

Seeing that Nahusha would not compromise, Shachi asked him for some time to think about his proposal. Nahusha acquiesced. In the meantime Shachi went to Brihaspati, the guru of gods, for shelter and advice. Brihaspati counseled her that the only one who could help her in this situation was Goddess Saraswati; so he initiated her into the worship of the Goddess. Shachi offered adorations to Goddess Saraswati, and the Goddess gave her insight about what to do. With her intellect touched by the grace of Goddess Saraswati, Shachi knew how to handle the situation.

She sent a message to Nahusha that she would accept him as her husband, but that he should come to her in a particular way. She expressed her view that every god had a special vehicle: Lord Vishnu rode on Garuda, Shiva on a bull, etc. Since he was a person from the mortal world who rose to such great power, he must have a unique vehicle. Her desire was that he should be brought to her on a palanquin carried by sages. No one had ever thought of that before. It would be indeed unique!

Nahusha, with his pride and tremendous ego, didn't realize that he was being tricked; rather, he felt that he was being honored. "Surely all the gods and sages adore me," his message stated. "Whatever I say they will do; so I shall come to you on a palanquin borne by sages."

And Shachi replied, "Very well, my lord, I shall await you."

Soon after this Nahusha chose a group of sages and asked them to bear the palanquin. They told him they would be happy to do it and smiled knowingly among themselves, for they knew what was waiting for Nahusha. Among them was the great Agastya, the most exalted of sages. There were others of great standing also. At the appointed time, the sages picked up the heavenly palanquin and hoisted it upon their shoulders for the journey to Shachi. Nahusha sat very proud as he eagerly awaited the moment when he would claim Shachi as his wife.

From the outset, however, Nahusha was annoyed with the sages because they weren't able to synchronize their movements and they moved much more slowly than he had expected. He sullenly thought to himself, "Lord Vishnu's vehicle moves a lot faster than mine. Come to think of it, everyone's vehicle moves faster. I made a big mistake to agree to this." In his impatience he scolded the sages, shouting, "*Sarpa, sarpa*—Quick, quick! Move faster!" His choice of words was most significant in this context, because the Sanskrit word, *sarpa*, has a double meaning: it can mean "quick" as well as "snake."

Nahusha's shouts to move faster caused the sages to quicken their pace to the extent that they could.

But their outpouring of effort and energy still didn't suit Nahusha. Screaming, "*Sarpa, sarpa!*" at the top of his lungs, the king lost his temper and kicked Agastya in the back as hard as he could. Agastya immediately cursed him: "May you become a *sarpa,* a snake!" So he turned into a snake that instant and fell from heaven down to the mortal world. There he remained for many centuries as a snake until he met King Yudhishthira at the time of the Mahabharata War.

Though a snake, he was still able to talk like a human being and thus was able to hold many interesting conversations with King Yudhishthira. Because of the contact he had with the great king, who was the embodiment of righteousness, his spirit was liberated; but in spite of this, he still had to go through a long process of suffering and degradation before this happened.

Mystic Meaning

This story symbolically portrays the rise and fall of ego, as represented by Nahusha. When a person performs *sakamya karmas,* or actions prompted by the desire for heavenly enjoyment, the fruit he reaps from doing such actions leads him to heavenly enjoyment. But enjoying that fruit of righteousness is not equivalent to attaining Liberation. King Nahusha was a great monarch who performed many good deeds, but as we saw, simply performing good deeds with no philosophical insight does not eliminate ego. And if ego is present, there will always be a basis for degradation.

The vast majority of people do not understand what the goal of life is. Many people perform good deeds, relatively speaking, according to their concept of what is good, because they think that doing so will get them to Heaven. But if you have philosophical insight you do not seek a reward in heaven; you seek the dissolution of ego itself. You perform actions for *chitta shudhi*, or purity of the heart, not for enjoyment on the astral plane.

Another point illustrated by the parable is that if the unconscious has not been purified—if real aspiration has not developed—then possessions, power, and glory all create a twisted intellect. If a person lacking purity of intellect attains great power he becomes swollen-headed. If you cannot handle power you will fall, and that is what happened to Nahusha.

Becoming a snake is symbolic of remaining in the realm of relativity—in a realm where there is karma and birth and death.

Shachi is the principle of pure intellect—which cannot be owned by ego. Any effort to dominate the intellect by an egoistic process is a movement that will lead one to degradation.

Yoking the sages to a palanquin also has mystical significance. When you have not brought order in your personality, it is like a runaway chariot. The chariot of your personality has to be driven by the higher principles of your soul such as understanding, reasoning and reflection—symbolized by the sages—not by your ego. But instead, the lesser in you tries to dominate the higher.

The right destination for the ego is that state wherein it is effaced. When ego allows itself to be effaced, there lies its exaltation, its grandeur. But when ego allows itself to be intensified, degradation results. This seems paradoxical, but therein lies the subtle mystery of mysticism: you enjoy existence more when your ego dissolves.

Thus, when Nahusha tried to dominate the sages he initiated his own downfall. Instead of possessing Shachi—the principle of purity, prosperity, and progress—his soul fell into a state of degradation and bondage.

Further, the story shows that by adoring Goddess Saraswati you allow your ego to be dominated by pure intellect. By making you reflective, Goddess allows you to have proper reasoning and insight. If you exalt your ego, however, and live for egoistic values—power, fame, glory, and wealth—then the same Goddess who can enlighten the intellect deludes it. This is the same process that caused Nahusha to fall. The Goddess in you is ever ready, either to delude your intellect, or to enlighten it.

When you turn towards egoistic feelings such as selfishness, greed, and vanity, the Saraswati within you smiles in a sinister way, causing your intellect to become gradually twisted. Though you may think that you are doing good to yourself, you are actually creating a basis for future sorrow. On the other hand, when you follow the path of righteousness and allow good qualities to develop, the Saraswati within you smiles in a heavenly way; and your intellect begins to recover its brilliance. You begin to understand the subtle secrets of life and discover the simplest way to transcend all your troubles and turmoils. This is the process in which intellect becomes intuitive. Figuratively speaking, your soul rushes toward the heavenly world. But when ego dominates, the soul rushes headlong down into the world-process.

May you receive the blessings of Goddess Saraswati!

About Swami Jyotirmayananda and His Ashram

Swami Jyotirmayananda was born on February 3, 1931, in a pious family in Dumari Buzurg, District Saran, Bihar, India—a northern province sanctified by the great Lord Buddha. From his early childhood he showed various marks of future saintliness. He was calm and reflective, compassionate to all, and a constant source of inspiration to all who came in contact with him. Side by side with his studies and practical duties, he reflected upon the deeper purpose of life.

An overwhelming feeling to serve humanity through a spiritual life led him to embrace the ancient order of *Sanyasa* on February 3, 1953, at the age of 22. Living in the Himalayan retreats by the sacred River Ganges, he practiced intense austerities. In tireless service of his Guru, Sri Swami Sivananda Maharaj, Swamiji taught at the Yoga Vedanta Forest Academy as a professor of religion. In addition to giving lectures on the Upanishads, Raja Yoga and all the important scriptures of India, he was the editor of the *Yoga Vedanta Journal*. Ever able to assist foreign students in their understanding of Yoga and Vedanta, his intuitive perception of their problems endeared him to all.

Swamiji's exemplary life, love towards all beings, great command of spiritual knowledge, and dynamic expositions on Yoga and Vedanta philosophy attracted enormous interest all over India. He frequently lectured by invitation at the All India Vedanta Conferences in Delhi, Amritsar, Ludhiana, and other parts of India.

In 1962, after many requests, Swami Jyotirmayananda came to the West to spread the knowledge of India. As founder of Sanatan Dharma Mandir in Puerto Rico (1962-1969), Swamiji rendered unique service to humanity through his regular classes, weekly radio lectures in English and in Spanish, and numerous TV appearances.

In March 1969, Swamiji moved to Miami, Florida, and established the Ashram that has become the center for the international activities of the Yoga Research Foundation. Branches of this organization now exist throughout the world, and spread the teachings of Yoga to aspirants everywhere.

In 1985, Swamiji founded the International Yoga Society ashram near New Delhi, India, and in 2000, another in Bihar, India.

The International Yoga Society serves the community through yoga classes, by publishing the Hindi journal, *Yoganjali,* and by operating free medical clinics, as well as the Bal Divya Jyoti Public School, and the Lalita Jyoti Anathalaya (orphanage).

Today Swami Jyotirmayananda occupies a place of the highest order among the international men of wisdom. He is well recognized as the foremost proponent of Integral Yoga, a way of life and thought that synthesizes the various aspects of the ancient Yoga tradition into a comprehensive plan of personality integration.

Through insightful lectures that bring inspiration to thousands who attend the conferences, camps and philosophical gatherings, Swamiji shares the range and richness of his knowledge of the great scriptures of the world.

His monthly magazine—*International Yoga Guide*—is enjoyed by spiritual seekers throughout the world. His numerous books, cassette tapes are enriching the lives of countless aspirants who have longed for spiritual guidance that makes the most profound secrets of Yoga available to them in a manner that is joyous and practical.

Despite the international scope of his activites, Swamiji still maintains an intimate setting at his main Ashram in Miami that allows fortunate aspirants to have the privilege of actually studying and working under his direct guidance. In the lecture hall of the Foundation, Swami Jyotirmayananda personally conducts an intense weekly schedule of classes on the Bhagavad Gita, Yoga Vasistha, Mahabharata, Raja Yoga, Upanishads, Panchadashi, the Bible, and meditation.

With a Work/Study Scholarship, qualified students are able to attend all classes conducted by Swamiji tuition-free. In return, students devote their energy and talents to the Foundation's noble mission.

The Yoga Research Foundation lies in the southwest section of Miami, five minutes from the University of Miami and 15 minutes from the Miami International Airport. The main Ashram is on a two and a half acre plot surrounded by trees and exotic plants, reminiscent of the forest hermitages of the ancient sages. In this serene yet dynamic environment, the holy presence of Swami Jyotirmayananda fills the atmosphere with the silent, powerful message of Truth, and the soul is nurtured and nourished, allowing for a total education and evolution of one's inner Self.

YRF Publications
by Swami Jyotirmayananda

Concentration and Meditation (cloth) 15.00
Applied Yoga (cloth) 15.00
Death and Reincarnation (cloth)................................... 15.00
Raja Yoga—Study of Mind (cloth) 15.00
Yoga Can Change Your Life 7.00
Yoga Guide.. 7.00
The Mystery of the Soul (Katha Upanishad) 5.00
The Way to Liberation (Mahabharata, 2 Vols., each 10.00
Yoga Vasistha, 6 Vols., each 10.00
Yoga Exercises for Health and Happiness 10.00
Mantra, Kirtana, Yantra, and Tantra................................ 6.00
Hindu Gods and Goddesses 6.00
Beauty and Health through Yoga Relaxation................... 4.00
Yoga Quotations 7.00
Yoga Mystic Poems 6.00
Yoga in Life.. 5.00
Yoga Mystic Stories 7.00
Yoga Stories and Parables.. 7.00
Raja Yoga Sutras... 7.00
Yoga Wisdom of the Upanishads 7.00
Yoga Secrets of Psychic Powers..................................... 7.00
Jnana Yoga (Yoga Secrets of Wisdom) 4.00
Vedanta in Brief 7.00
Sex-Sublimation, Truth and Non-Violence 7.00
Yoga of Perfection (Srimad Bhagavad Gita).................... 7.00
Waking, Dream and Deep Sleep 4.00
Integral Yoga—A Primer Course 5.00
Yoga Essays for Self-Improvement 7.00
The Yoga of Divine Love 7.00
Integral Yoga Today... 4.00
Yoga of Enlightenment (Gita—Chapter 18) 4.00
Advice to Householders 6.00
The Glory of Lord Krishna (Mysticism of Srimad Bhagavatam)19.00
Mysticism of Mahabharata 10.00
Mysticism of Ramayana 12.00
Worship of God as Mother—Mysticism of Devi Mahatmya 14.00
The Art of Positive Thinking... 12.00
The Art of Positive Feeling 10.00
The Four Gatekeepers at the Palace of Liberation 5.00

(All prices subject to change)

Enjoy 12 full months of Yoga's finest with Swami Jyotirmayananda's unique magazine— INTERNATIONAL YOGA GUIDE

Enter your subscription to International Yoga Guide and get a year's worth of instruction and guidance—a year's worth of intriguing, thought-provoking reading. Month by month come fresh articles, new ideas, and the innovative style that has made Swami Jyotirmayananda's Integral Yoga renowned the world over.

Subscribe now! Along with insightful essays about applying Integral Yoga in your daily life, you'll find articles on:

- Meditation
- Classic Literature
- Questions & Answers
- Exercise
- Spiritual Instructions

When you subscribe to International Yoga Guide: you automatically become a member of the Yoga Research Foundation.

All standing member/subscribers are entitled to the following privileges and benefits:

10% discount on all cassettes and book orders

50% off all IYG back issues

Personal correspondence with Swami Jyotirmayananda on any question or difficulty

Special Lecture Series
by Swami Jyotirmayananda

1 hr lectures Cassette-$10 CD-$12 DVD-$25
(All prices subject to change)

3001	How to Handle Stress
3002	How to Promote Relaxation
3003	Karma & Reincarnation
3004	The Way to Liberation
3005	How to Face Death
3006	How to Develop Faith
3007	How to Face Adversity
3008	Insight into Karma Yoga
3009	Harmony in Human Relation
3010	Insight into Bhakti Yoga
3011	Insight into Jnana Yoga
3012	The Art of Positive Living
3013	The Art of Handling the Ego
3014	Insight into Raja Yoga
3015	The Essence of the Gita
3016	The Power of Prayer
3017	The Quest for Happiness
3018	Insight into Kundalini Yoga
3019	Insight into Dharma
3020	God as Mother
3021	The Philosophy of Maya
3022	Insight into Integral Yoga
3023	The Message of Moses
3024	The Message of Buddha
3025	How to Overcome Fear
3026	Philosophy of Non-violence
3027	Educating the Unconscious
3028	Quest for Peace
3029	Ascending Heights of Samadhi
3030	Insight into the Three Modes of Nature
3031	Insight into the Great Utterances of the Veda
3032	The Message of Lord Jesus
3033	Qualities that Enrich Your Life
3034	Insight into Psychic Powers
3035	Insight into the Power of Speech

3036	Insight into Mantra Yoga
3037	How to Develop Willpower
3038	Overcome Prejudice
3039	Insight into Fate and Free Will
3040	Sadhana in Jnana Yoga
3041	Sadhana in Raja Yoga
3042	Sadhana in Bhakti Yoga
3043	Sadhana in Karma Yoga
3044	Sadhana in Integral Yoga
3045	Insight into Om
3046	Insight into Kriya Yoga
3047	Unity of Religions
3048	Importance of Satsanga
3049	Insight into Intuition
3050	Insight into Renunciation
3051	The Practice of Equanimity
3052	The Art of Positive Feeling
3053	The Practice of Meditation in Raja Yoga
3054	Meditation in Bhakti Yoga
3055	Meditation in Jnana Yoga
3056	Insight into Self-effort
3057	Enquiry into "Who Am I?"
3058	The Peace Chants of the Upanishads
3059	Insight into Spiritual Strength
3060	Success in Sadhana
3061	Insight into Surrender to God
3062	The Characteristics of Enlightenment
3063	The Art of Cheerfulness
3064	The Philosophy of Time
3065	Self-effort and Grace
3066	The Art of Positive Thinking
3067	The Quality of Contentment
3068	Insight into God-realization
3069	The Quality of Goodness
3070	The Practice of Non-violence
3071	Insight into Liberation
3072	Insight into Tantra Yoga
3073	Insight into Maya
3074	Five States of the Mind
3075	From Sorrow to Sunshine

3076	From Darkness to Light
3077	The Quality of Serenity
3078	The Wisdom of the Vedas
3079	Insight into Bondage & Release
3080	The Mystic Art of Detachment
3081	The Mysteries of the Mind
3082	Insight into the Cessation of Pain
3083	Insight into Divine Worship
3084	The Journey After Death
3085	Insight into Austerity
3086	The Quality of Viveka (Discrimination)
3087	Insight into Vairagya
3088	Insight into the 3 Gunas of Nature
3089	Insight into Purity of Feeling
3090	The Quality of Fortitude
3091	The Practice of Truthfulness
3092	Quality of Compassion
3094	Insight into Om Tat Sat
3095	Karma & Reincarnation
3096	The Quality of Moderation
3097	Insight into Satsanga
3098	Insight into Bhuma
3099	Mysticism of the Avataras-Pt.1
3100	Mysticism of the Avataras-Pt.2
3101	Mysticism of the Avataras – Pt. 3
3102	Insight into Tat Twam Asi
3103	The Path After Death
3104	Insight into Upasana (Devout Meditation)
3105	Insight into Abhyasa (Repeated Effort)
3106	How to Overcome Hatred
3107	The Seven Steps of Wisdom
3108	Insight into Parabhakti
3109	Austerity of the Mind
3110	Means to Self-realization
3111	Insight into Purity of Body & Mind
3112	Insight into Divine Grace
3113	Practice of Reflection or Manana
3114	Niddidhyasana (Vedantic Meditation)
3115	Insight into Sakshatkara (Self-realization)
3116	Peace and Harmony in the World

3117	Insight into Equal Vision
3118	The Mystic Art of Divine Surrender
3119	How to Enrich Your Life
3120	Harmony in Daily Life
3121	Insight into the Nine Modes of Devotion
3122	The Story of Lila
3123	The Story of King Lavana
3124	The Fight between Good and Evil
3125	Wisdom of the Vedas
3126	Insight into the Kleshas
3127	Interdependence of Bhakti and Jnana
3128	The Virtue of Patience
3129	The Divine Plan of Life
3130	Seek the Kingdom of Heaven
3131	The Quality of Charity
3132	The Path of Blessedness
3133	Insight into Faith & Reason

...and many more titles upon request

From 1969 to the present, Swami Jyotirmayananda has given complete lecture series on Yoga Vasistha, Bhagavad Gita, Avadhuta Gita, Bible, Raja Yoga Sutras, Narada Bhakti Sutras, Shandilya Bhakti Sutras, Devi Mahatmya, Ramayana, Mahabharata, Bhagavat Purana, Jivan Mukti Viveka, Panchadashi, Viveka Chudamani, and the major and minor Upanishads. All of these scriptural lectures are available on cassette or CD upon request. In addition there are hundreds of other poignant topics of Yoga philosophy available. Please contact us for more information at 305-666-2006.